UNDERSTANDI
BUDDHISM

UNDERSTANDING BUDDHISM

Key Themes

HEINRICH DUMOULIN

Translated and adapted from the German
by Joseph S. O'Leary

New York WEATHERHILL Tokyo

First edition, 1994

Published by Weatherhill, Inc., 420 Madison Avenue, 15th Floor, New York, New York, 10017. Printed in the United States.

Cover design by Liz Trovato, incorporating a painting of a bodhisattva from the caves of Dunhuang.

Library of Congress Cataloging-in-Publication Data

Dumoulin, Heinrich.
[Begegnung mit dem Buddhismus. English]
Understanding Buddhism : key themes / by Heinrich Dumoulin ; translated and adapted by Joseph S. O'Leary.—1st Weatherhill ed.
p. cm.
Includes bibliographical references and index.
ISBN 0-8348-0297-X : $14.95
1. Buddhism. I. O'Leary, Joseph Stephen. II. Title.
BQ4015.D8413 1993
294.3—dc20 93-29191
CIP

Contents

UNDERSTANDING BUDDHISM

EDITOR'S NOTE: All foreign words, whether or not they appear in English dictionaries, are italicized on first appearance only but written with all diacritic markings on every appearance.

I

The Historic Opportunity

At the level of philosophical and theological reflection, as well as in the practical cultivation of a spiritual life, the Buddhist tradition holds out to Westerners today a fascinating challenge and a horizon of unequaled promise. If the challenge is not met and the promise not realized, it is usually because people stumble over certain apparent absurdities in the Buddhist message, or are discouraged by a stereotyped and impoverished notion of what Buddhism stands for. Some see Buddhism as a pessimistic religion, preaching hostility to everyday life and holding out as the highest ideal a condition of pure nihilistic extinction. Others see it as crushing and erasing the reality of the individual human person. The Buddha's silence about God troubles others, who see it as the mark of a bleakly impersonal atheism or pantheism. An allied impression is that Buddhism is a cold rationalism, excluding all recourse to faith, and that love and compassion cannot really flourish in this climate.

My hope is to provide an antidote for these misunderstandings—for such they are—in the following pages. To do so I turn back from the

Zen tradition, to which I have devoted a great part of my life's work,[1] and take up some of the most basic and central Buddhist topics, chiefly concerning the status of the human person in Buddhist thought and practice. I shall deal with the doctrine of non-self against the background of the Buddha's teaching of the Four Noble Truths as found in the Pali Canon. Then, in discussing the rational character of Buddhist thought and its cult of a supreme wisdom, I shall draw attention to the place of faith in the Buddhist tradition, which has often been underestimated. The chapters on compassion and meditation will bring out the human profile of these central Buddhist activities, drawing comparisons with the highly personalized charity and prayer of the Christian tradition. Turning to the question of God, I shall dwell on the enigmatic silence with which the Buddha responded to metaphysical questions, and show that this can be seen as one of several ways in which Buddhism gives witness to divine transcendence. Finally, I shall draw on religious and artistic sources to show that Buddhism does not lack a refined sense of individual human personhood.[2]

Within each chapter, I shall follow the chronological development from the message of the Buddha himself through the philosophical elaborations of the Abhidharma, and then on through the sūtras, philosophies, and varied schools of Mahāyāna Buddhism. Contemporary Buddhologists distinguish three phases in the history of the religion. The original teaching of the Buddha and his disciples eludes precise definition, but is rightly taken to contain the entirety of Buddhism *in nuce*. All the key themes of Buddhist thought point back to this original matrix. Next, the early Buddhist centuries gave rise to a number of schools which played a capital role in the development of Buddhist doctrine. These flourished in Northwest India and Central Asia, but withered away for various reasons during the first millennium CE, except for Theravāda, which is still a living religion in Sri Lanka, Burma, Thailand, Cambodia, and Laos. Lastly, Mahāyāna, the "Greater Vehicle," which emerged during the first century BCE and the first century CE, and spread chiefly in East Asia, includes a great number of quite divergent currents, each bringing its own accentuation to the major Buddhist themes. The Mahāyānists dubbed the previous form of Buddhism Hīnayāna, or the "Lesser Vehicle," a pejorative title I shall try to avoid. In current usage, the negative connotations of the term "Hīnayāna" are avoided by calling it "Hearers' Vehicle" (Sanskrit: Śrāvakayāna). Robert Thurman uses "Individual Vehicle" and "Universal Vehicle" for Hīnayāna and Mahāyāna respectively.[3]

My hope is that the discussion of the selected key themes will help remove stumbling blocks that have prevented Western and especially Christian inquirers from participating as fully as they might in what I consider to be one of the greatest spiritual and intellectual adventures of our time. In this introductory chapter I shall portray the present privileged moment of encounter with Buddhism against its historical background. Though Buddhism and Christianity have been mighty spiritual forces in the world for the past two thousand years, it is only in this century that they have come to discover one another in a real and deep way, and it is only in recent decades that the barriers to mutual understanding have begun to collapse. A look back at three previous moments of encounter, all ending in failure and disappointment, can help us understand the privileged character of the present historic opportunity.

The East-West Encounter in Antiquity

Eastern spirituality first affected the West when Alexander the Great (who led an army of one hundred twenty thousand in the expedition of 327 BCE) and his successors brought Hellenistic culture to the Kabul valley and over the Indus river to the region of Gandhāra. Here Buddhist monks, dwelling in spacious stone monasteries, first came to know Western culture from their contacts with huge and motley armies drawn not only from the Roman and Greek populations but from all parts of the Mediterranean and Asia Minor. The art generated by this cultural interaction—known as Indo-Greek art or the art of Gandhāra[4]—spread far to the west from its center Taxila and flourished for a period of some five hundred years, until it was finally destroyed by the invasion of the White Huns in the fifth century CE. Extensive excavations have brought to light many splendid works of this period, and today the statues, Buddha heads, and stūpa remnants of Gandhāra are an object of wonder to both archaeologists and tourists. The combination of Indian motifs with those of late antiquity conveys a sense of a mighty intermingling of peoples and cultures, a transfusion that anticipates what is taking place in our own day. This impression is reinforced by the fact that the Gandhāra style, representing the intersection of two lines—one from India, the other from Greece—spread eastward to Central Asia and to China, where it was transformed into something specifically East Asian. Its distinctive traits still shimmer through in the Korean and Japanese works which represent the most remote point in its transmission.

Egypt was the site of another meeting of Eastern and Western culture, on a lesser scale. In the great cultural melting pot of Alexandria, during the centuries before and after Christ, people eagerly absorbed influences not only from the Middle East but also from India. Though we know of the presence of Indian saints or ascetics, their precise religious affiliation cannot be established. Clement of Alexandria (c. 150–between 211 and 215) was the first Western writer to name "a certain Buddha whom, because of his great virtues, the Indians honor as a god" (*Stromateis* I 15). If we examine such sources as Jewish philosophy (Philo), Jewish sects such as the Essenes, Gnostic circles, and also the early Christian congregations, we find reason to believe that the impact of Indian spirituality was felt in the land of the Nile and eventually spread to the entire Hellenistic world. However, no instance of direct influence in a particular case has yet been established with certitude.

A real encounter implies influence in both directions. What Buddhism received from contact with Greece is too evident to be missed. A Buddhist influence on Western intellectual life and especially on early Christianity has been surmised especially in two areas. The first of these is monasticism. Was there an Indian, or specifically a Buddhist influence at work in the movement whereby, during the early centuries of Eastern Christianity, anchorites who dwelt in the wilderness organized themselves into monastic communities in Egypt, Syria, the Sinai Peninsula, and Mount Athos? This cannot be proved. Yet it is a tempting explanation for the affinities that are recognized with astonishment by Western monks whenever they encounter the lifestyle of their counterparts, the *bhikkhu* and *bhikkhunī* (monks and nuns) in Buddhist countries. Thomas Merton (1915–68) is the best-known example of a Western monk thus powerfully drawn by Buddhist monastic culture and meditation.

The other area most suggestive of Indian or Buddhist influence is that of mysticism. Nowhere is Christianity closer to Buddhism than in the teachings of spiritual masters on the negative way, teachings elaborated into an apophatic theology (*theologia negativa*) by Pseudo-Dionysius (early sixth century). Apophatic theology consists in the thoroughgoing negation of all concepts and categories in respect to the divine being, which it speaks of in negative terms. It made its first appearance in the West about the beginning of the Christian era in Philo (first to second century CE), the Neo-Pythagoreans, and the Gnostic schools. As the fourth-century Arian controversy drew to its close, the ineffability and incomprehensibility of God were strongly affirmed by Gregory of Nazianzus (c. 330–c. 389), Gregory of Nyssa (c. 335–c. 394), and John Chrysostom (c. 347–c. 407). These great theologians provided a solid basis for the thought of Pseudo-Dionysius, who also drew heavily on the thought of the Neo-Platonist philosopher Proclus (410?–85).

Are the similarities between Eastern and Western mysticism due exclusively to a convergence on the level of spiritual experience, or was Christian negative theology prompted by an encounter with Asia? There has been much discussion of possible Indian influences on the Middle Platonic and Neo-Platonic ideas which these theologians had absorbed, particularly in connection with Plotinus's mysticism of the One. Émile Bréhier spoke of the orientalism of Plotinus and of deep affinities between certain central aspects of Plotinian doctrine and the *Upanishads*.[5] It is hard to dismiss the belief that the stream of negative theology, preserved and expanded in Christian mystical thought down to the present time, has one of its sources in that distant encounter with a form of Indian spirituality closely related to Buddhism.

Though the channels of interaction remain obscure, these early interactions between Eastern and Western spirituality are a haunting theme in the history of religions and loom in the background of the present encounter between Buddhism and Christianity.

Nestorian Christianity in China

Well documented, in contrast, is the second major religious encounter between East and West, which took place in the middle ages, when Nestorian Christians traveled from the Middle East through Central Asia into China. Their arrival in China is dated 631, and their presence is still attested in the fourteenth century. They had a place of worship in Ch'ang-an, the radiant capital of T'ang-dynasty China (618–c. 907), where, along with small Manichean, Zoroastrian, and Islamic communities, they added to the interreligious flavor of the predominantly Buddhist and Taoist city. The inscription on the memorial stone of Hsinanfu, the so-called Nestorian Stone, erected jointly by Christians and Buddhists in 781, attests to the bonds of close friendship that were formed between these Nestorian Christians and the Buddhists. The text reveals that the Christians had adapted themselves more to Buddhism than the Buddhists had to Christianity. From the fact that the inscription recounts at length the life of Christ but makes no mention of the crucifixion, the English historian Charles Eliot concludes that Nestorian Christianity in China had surrendered the doctrine of the Atonement.[6]

As to the possibility of Christian influence on Buddhism, the form of Buddhism that most suggests such an influence is the Pure Land school, centered on a savior figure, the Buddha Amitābha ("of infinite light") or Amitāyus ("of infinite life"), better known today by the Japanese form of the name, Amida. A Christian influence on Amidism could not have come from the Nestorians, for this movement was already fully formed by the time of the Nestorians' arrival in China. The basic elements are already contained in the two fundamental Pure Land sūtras, probably composed in India in the second century. Historians of religion explain the quasi-monotheistic features of the Buddha Amitābha by reference to the milieu in which the cult emerged. The imagery of light seems to come from Iran and the devotionalism stems from the Indian *bhakti* piety. Nevertheless, it is not impossible that certain traits of the Amida religion which are strikingly reminiscent of Christianity, such as faith, trusting surrender, and meditative recollection, were heightened as a result of intimate commerce between the Nestorian Christians and Chinese devotees of Amida. Though one must be prudent in postulating direct influences, it remains possible that Amida Buddhism owes its religious power in East Asia to some extent to the long neighborly coexistence of Amida devotees and the Nestorians in China. Apart from the question of historical influence, the general resemblances between Pure Land and Christianity have fascinated several modern Christian theologians.[7]

In the final phase of the early Christian-Buddhist encounters in China occurred the Asian journeys of the Franciscan missionaries (thirteenth and fourteenth centuries) and of the Venetian explorer Marco Polo (ca.1254–1324). Their reports indicate great efforts to maintain the favorable climate which they found at the Mongolian emperor's court in Peking. The Franciscans were impressed by the strict ascetic lives of the Buddhist monks, and wrote home in admiration of their barefoot begging and their continence. This high praise allows us to infer that their relations with the Buddhists were cordial ones, which makes all the more regrettable the sudden and complete end of this relationship with the fall of the Yüan dynasty in the second half of the fourteenth century.

Let us listen to the Franciscan William of Rubrouck (c. 1215–c. 1295) reporting on his mission of 1253–55:

> The priests (in the country of the Uighurs) keep their heads uncovered as long as they are in the temple, reading in silence, a

silence strictly maintained. When I entered a certain temple and found them sitting in this way, I tried in many ways to provoke them to speech, but could by no means do so. . . . When I saw their many idols, small and great, I asked them what they themselves believed about God. They answered: "We believe in only one God." And I asked: "Do you believe him to be spirit or something corporeal?" They said: "We believe he is spirit." "Do you believe that at one time he took human nature?" "Not at all." "If you believe him to be one and to be spirit, why do you make corporeal images, and so many of them? And since you don't believe God was made man, why do use images of humans rather than of some other animal?" They replied: "We do not consider these images of God, but they are memorials of deceased human beings." Then they asked me, as if in derision: "Where is God?" I returned: "Where is your soul?" "In our body." "Isn't it everywhere in your body, governing it all, and yet is unseen? So God is everywhere, and governs everything, yet is invisible because he is wisdom and intelligence." Then when I wanted to argue about many things, my exhausted interpreter, unable to express my thoughts, made me stop.[8]

The Encounter with Zen Buddhists in Japan

A third encounter of Buddhists and Christians took place in Japan at the beginning of the modern period. On the Buddhist side the most prominent role was taken by the Zen school.[9] Soon after his landing in Kagoshima, Francis Xavier (1506–52), the first Christian missionary in Japan, visited a Zen temple and formed a warm friendship with the aged abbot Ninshitsu (d. 1556). His conversations with his Buddhist friend are remarkable for their noble, generous humanity and as an interreligious exchange of ideas. Xavier asked the Zen abbot which period in life he regarded as better, youth or old age. Ninshitsu opted for youth, when the body is still free from sickness and one is free to act as one desires. Xavier countered this with an edifying image: "At what point do the passengers on a ship experience the greatest happiness: when they are still in mid-ocean and exposed to wind, waves and storm, or when they approach the harbor which brings rest from all the dangers of storm and shipwreck?" Ninshitsu frankly replied: "I know the harbor is more pleasing to those who are crossing the bar, but since it is not yet clear to me, and I have not decided which is the better harbor, I do not know where or how I should put to shore." Considering the immense cultural and linguistic gap, this is a remarkable success in communication "from heart to heart." On the basis of such experiences Xavier thought it possible for Christian missionaries to engage in religious disputations with Buddhist monks. For, as he writes in a letter to Europe, "the Japanese have a sharp understanding and pay great heed to reason."

The Portuguese Jesuit Cosme de Torres was also noted for his enthusiasm for such debates, to which he brought an unshakable trust in the power of reason. He writes: "When you convey the truth to their understanding through rational explanations, they forget their idols and become Christians immediately." Extensive reports of his discussions with Buddhist monks from the Zen school in Yamaguchi have been transmitted to us.[10] The debate was impassioned, but unsuccessful. The missionary, famed for his talent and erudition, sought to convince his Eastern dialogue partners of the existence of God, using scholastic arguments, while the Buddhists tirelessly repeated the difficult axioms of Mahāyāna philosophy and spoke with enthusiasm of its central doctrine of emptiness (Sanskrit: *śūnyatā;* Japanese: *kū*) or nothingness (Japanese: *mu*). The failure of the conversations was due above all to the Jesuit theologian's understanding of the Buddhist teaching as nihilistic and his failure to recognize the mystical character of the negative formulations.

These scenes prompt reflection on the gaps separating different cultural and linguistic horizons, and the need for the kind of hermeneutical sensitivity for which Raimundo Panikkar pleads:

> A word is not totally separable from the meaning we give to it and each of us in fact gives different shades of meaning to the same word. A word reflects a total human experience and cannot be

> severed from it. A word is not empirically or logically detectable. When we say "justice," "dharma," "karunā," we cannot point to an object, but have to refer to a crystallization of human experiences that vary with people, places, ages, etc. We cannot properly speaking translate words. . . . There is not an object "God," "justice," or "Brahman," a thing in itself independent of those living words, over against which we may check the correctness of the translation. . . . The translation of religious insights cannot be done unless the insight that has originated that word is also transplanted.[11]

If the three Western encounters with Buddhism which we have discussed—one ancient, one medieval, and one modern—in each case stopped half-way, despite the intensity of interest on the Western side and the friendship shown in return by the Asian partner, the blockage must stem from a profound mutual incomprehension preventing any real inner accord from being realized. Many of the barriers are due to a fixation on certain patterns of thoughts and language and a failure to interpret the total life context out of which Buddhist words and representations emerge. In this work I shall attempt to trace the main Buddhist themes, which have been a stumbling block to understanding in the past, back to their existential matrix. They will lose nothing of their foreignness in this process, but their affinity with the existential roots of Western religion and philosophy will make itself felt in a way that secures a foothold for a dialogue that can no longer be broken off.

THE SITUATION TODAY

In view of the abortive encounters of the past the prospects for a new Buddhist-Christian encounter seemed, up to only a few years ago, distinctly discouraging. The cultured public, inadequately informed, generally took it for granted that the atheistic or pantheistic character of Buddhism, with its nihilistic ideal of final extinction, was fundamentally opposed to Christianity, which is based on a historical revelation and affirms the existence of a transcendent God and an immortal soul.

Those who were drawn to Eastern wisdom, especially meditation and mysticism, often thought they could embark on an Asian spiritual journey only at the price of turning their back on Christianity.

Now we do not intend to assert that there are no radical differences between Buddhism and Christianity. Nor do we want to create the impression that dialogue with Buddhists is a simple affair promising quick results; the mutual understanding envisaged in such dialogue requires the most strenuous persistence. Nonetheless, the breaking of the deadlock in Buddhist-Christian relations has set off a process of mutual discovery which has a momentum of its own, sweeping Christians along with it at an accelerating pace, and drawing them irresistibly into new perspectives of religious thought, even while certain basic issues still remain unresolved.

Great changes in the global situation have facilitated this eagerness for interreligious dialogue. Dialogue has become a necessity not only for harmonious coexistence and cooperation between people of different religious cultures, but for the more basic reason that the questions that haunt people of all cultures cannot be satisfactorily addressed if the interreligious horizon is closed off. These questions were listed by Vatican II as follows:

> What is man? What is the meaning and purpose of life? What is upright behavior, and what is sinful? Where does suffering originate, and what end does it serve? How can genuine happiness be found? What happens at death? What is judgment? What reward follows death? And finally, what is the ultimate mystery, beyond human explanation, which embraces our entire existence, from which we take our origin and towards which we tend?[12]

Today, more and more aware of the unity of humanity and the limitations of the earth's resources, we discuss with new urgency and concreteness the sense of the human project and the fate of the earth, sometimes in a mood verging on the apocalyptic, and we cast about for a wisdom that goes beyond the dominance of the technological. Out of this sense of crisis has grown a new religious consciousness which seeks convincing answers, and in this quest Asian spirituality, particularly Buddhism, has become an indispensable reference.

On the Eastern side too, the necessity of an interior spiritual communication with the West is felt. Without it, there is a technological yoking together of the hemispheres, but their solidarity in a single global community cannot be well articulated. A purely secular engagement with Western philosophy and ethics, which abstracts from religious traditions and their problems, is scarcely practicable, nor can Asian worldviews be explained to the West without attention to their pervasive religious connotations. The encounter of cultures carries an inalienable religious dimension, which can be dealt with only in philosophical and interreligious dialogue.

Perhaps even more than the changed world situation, the radicalized theological questioning of our time has favored the breakthroughs in the dialogue between Christianity and Buddhism. Theological insight has brought our understanding of the religious situation of humanity to a threshold where full-scale dialogue between the religions becomes a possibility for the first time. These new ways of looking at things have created capacious frameworks for Christian-Buddhist discussion, which in turn is further broadening the basic categories of theology.

The present rediscovery of Buddhism already has a history of more than a century behind it. As one sample of the excitement it has generated let us listen to what a far-sighted theologian and inspiring teacher, Romano Guardini, wrote in 1937:

> There is only one figure who invites us to place him in proximity to Jesus: the Buddha. This man is an immense riddle. He stands in a frightening, almost superhuman freedom; yet the goodness he exudes is as a cosmic power. The Buddha will perhaps be the last one with whom Christianity will have to work out a relationship. None has yet identified his Christian significance. Perhaps, in addition to John, the last bearer of Hebrew prophetic tradition, Christ has another Precursor from the heart of antique culture,

> Socrates, and yet a third who has spoken the last word of Eastern religious insight and overcoming, the Buddha.
>
> The domain of human achievement is limited to this world. One only has sought to put his hand on Being itself: the Buddha. He desired more than mere betterment, or a peace found in leaving the world behind. He undertook the inconceivable: taking his stand in human existence, to lift existence itself from its hinges. What he meant by nirvāṇa—the ultimate awakening, the cessation of illusion and of being—no one has yet been able to grasp or assess from a Christian point of view.[13]

These are deeply touching words. Yet their tone is rather remote from our more prosaic contemporary attitudes. We are less anxious to unveil ultimate mysteries. Our concern is less to identify the place of the Buddha in a Christian world view than to interpret the rich Buddhist heritage on its own terms. If the person of the Buddha still baffles our understanding, we seek to bring him into perspective less through lofty theological generalizations than through a study of the Buddhist event, the spiritual facts of Buddhism, as deployed in history.

The major breakthrough in Buddhist-Christian dialogue happened at the end of the Second World War, a moment at which the world religions found themselves challenged to contribute to the quest for peace and unity among nations, and to cooperate with one another. A new relationship of friendship was formed between the religions, an atmosphere of openness and sympathy, not to be measured by statistics but evident in the zeal with which they collaborated in their service of the world. Representatives of the world religions participated more actively in numerous congresses and conferences aiming at a unified world in the social, cultural, and scientific realms. A landmark event was Vatican II's *Declaration on the Relation of the Church to Non-Christian Religions,* which opens with the following words:

> In this age of ours, when men are drawing more closely together and the bonds of friendship between different peoples are being

> strengthened, the Church examines with greater care the relation which she has to non-Christian religions.

With remarkable breadth of vision, the Council exhorts the faithful

> to enter with prudence and charity into discussion and collaboration with members of other religions. Let Christians, while witnessing to their own faith and way of life, acknowledge, preserve and encourage the spiritual and moral truths found among non-Christians, also their social life and culture.[14]

This declaration did not remain a dead letter, but gave birth to bold initiatives which are still continuing.

The friendly climate thus established, fruitful as it was at the level of praxis, was only the precondition for full-scale interreligious dialogue. Moving from a benevolent respect for the religious values of Buddhism to an effort to penetrate and adopt the deepest insights of Buddhist tradition, Christians found themselves involved in an ecumenism of unprecedented scope and depth. The intra-Christian ecumenical movement had been led by the desire for church unity, highly prized in the New Testament sources but tragically lost in the course of history. The wider interreligious ecumenism has never entertained the aim of uniting all existing religions in a single world religion. The syncretism this would imply is incompatible with the Christian sense of identity and with that of other religions as well. In place of such a mirage of unification, the interreligious dialogue has above all stressed respect for the difference of the other.

The delicate problems such openness raises have become the theme of a new discipline, the theology of religions, which drew encouragement from the Council's teaching on the salvation of non-Christians and on religious freedom, a teaching that dissolved the inhibiting exclusivism of the earlier slogans: "no salvation outside the Church" and "error has no rights." The affirmation of religious freedom, based on respect for the personal dignity of every human being, has had the effect of undermining suspicious or dismissive attitudes towards other religious traditions, and it has provided a strong motivation for discovering and appreciating the positive worth of these traditions. This welcoming attitude to the other is now beginning to spread beyond the strict confines of the theology of religions to pervade the whole of Christian theology.

For an Existential Dialogue

As Buddhism established a niche for itself in European scholarship during the nineteenth century, it was subjected to methods of analysis begotten by Enlightenment rationalism. Attention was focused on the form of Buddhism practiced in the colonies of Ceylon (Sri Lanka) and Burma, namely Theravāda ("Learning of the Elders"), the only still-thriving school from among the score or so of schools into which early Buddhism had been divided before the rise of Mahāyāna. Scholars were attracted by the appeal of the living culture of the Theravāda countries, and by the high literary quality of the Theravāda scriptures, the Pali Canon, published along with English translations by the Pali Text Society, which made this the best known and the most influential form of Buddhism in the English-speaking world. A remarkable side effect of this Western interest was that it sparked off a Buddhist revival in Asia, giving Buddhists new confidence in the scientific value and contemporary pertinence of their beliefs. At first manifested chiefly in scholarship, the impulse given by this revival is still felt in renewal and modernization movements.

The discipline of the History of Religions gathered the fruits of research into its universe of knowledge, and systematic ordering and analysis took the form of Comparative Religion, in which analogies between religions were pursued with unbounded enthusiasm. Rites and ceremonies as well as regulations for religious behavior and monastic discipline provided a rich field for tracing analogies at the external level. Considerable attention was given to the thought-provoking similarities between the legend of the Buddha and the story of Jesus. In this context there arose an extensive literature on "Buddhism and Christianity." Today we can distinguish three phases or levels in this comparativist period: one which focused on external, superficial similarities; one which developed rational comparisons of doctrines and concepts; and one which examined experiences and existential attitudes with a view to reaching down to the deeper significance of the data. When this comparativist method tried to progress from analogies to questions of historical dependence, however, it ran into dead ends.

Of the three types of comparativism, the first is of least interest to the present Buddhist-Christian encounter. It has a particularly rich target in the legend of Barlaam and Josaphat, the Christianized version of a life of the Buddha originally written in Sanskrit, which was disseminated in various languages in the early Christian period. The names of "Saints" Barlaam and Josaphat were inserted in the *Martyrologium Romanum,* and there is a church in Palermo consecrated to them. Doubts about their authenticity surfaced only in the seventeenth century, when the Portuguese historian Diego do Conto pointed to the striking similarities to the story of the Buddha. The name Joasaph (the Greek form) derives from "bodhisattva" (a "being of wisdom," an epithet for the Buddha in his former lives) via Budasaf and Judasaf (Arabic); Barlaam probably comes from the name of an Indian ascetic, Bilahaur. The Barlaam-Josaphat legend covers large parts of the Buddha's life, with special emphasis on the conversion of the prince and his later monastic career. That the Christian world accepted the Buddha without resistance as a saint testifies to the resemblance between the Buddhist and the Christian ideals of holiness. Further confirmation of this may be found in the ironic fact that the Barlaam-Josaphat legend was later translated from the Latin into Chinese and Japanese, and was transmitted to new Japanese Christians as Christian hagiography.

The second style of comparativism dealt with conceptual and doctrinal resemblances and differences. Despite the great acumen of its practitioners and the undoubted value of their work, this method remains unsatisfactory for various reasons. Prescinding from personal spirituality and theological commitment in favor of a narrow concern with conceptual constructions, it was more convincing when it found oppositions than when it attempted to build bridges. It forgot that the encounter of religions does not proceed on the plane of pure doctrines, but has to do with human beings who speak with one another, understand one another, and learn from one another. Until this dimension of personal experience came into play, a true interreligious encounter was impossible.

In the third phase one seeks to be led by experiential apprehension of the religious data, leaving behind apologetic skirmishing and claims of superiority, in a shared quest for deeper understanding of what the religions intend to say. To practice this method, we must overcome the sense of embarrassment about having recourse to experience, felt not only by rationalist philosophers of religion but also, for a long time, by Catholic theologians fearful that talk of experience lessened the value of faith. We must trace the religious world to its basis in the existential and historical experience of humanity. Considered in abstraction from this experience, different religious systems are alien to each other and a source of division and conflict; recalled to their experiential roots, they are seen to be alternative explorations of our shared human destiny. It often happens that what seem sharp contradictions at the level of explicit doctrine are softened when this living context becomes apparent.

Christianity is centered in faith in the Gospel message of the Kingdom of God; Buddhism is centered in insight into the nature of suffering and liberation. Both religions permit an experience of the ultimate, highest reality, to which they invite one to open oneself by a conversion of mind. In Asian religion, just as this ultimate reality lies beyond words, so does the state of the mind that is in touch with it. Hence the importance of silence and of negative forms of speech, such as we also find in Christian negative theology. Words such as "emptiness" and "nothingness" point to the ultimate reality. In Christian negative theology there is a positive or kataphatic series of utterances which operates in tandem with the negative or apophatic one; both are based on scripture and were developed by such great theologians as Gregory of Nyssa, Augustine of Hippo (354–430), and Thomas Aquinas (1224–74). God is believed to have communicated himself in his revelation; his essence, however, remains ineffable. It lies beyond all concepts and determinations, and can as well be described in terms of not being as of being, since it is at once the fullness of every perfection and the nothingness beyond being.

In Buddhism, the royal road to the experience of ultimate reality is the practice of meditation. Whether the practitioner sits in the lotus position or repeats the holy name innumerable times before an image of the Buddha, his basic desire is to break through his conscious ego and come in touch with that genuine reality which is the goal from which the entire Buddhist religion acquires its meaning and function. It is of little importance what he calls that reality. An elderly Amida devotee whom I met in his temple on a lonely mountain top in a quiet corner of Japan once said to me, as if unsealing a secret: "Amida, you know, is emptiness." He had inwardly experienced Amida Buddha as emptiness, as the nothing beyond being, or as the fullness of nothing.

II

Suffering, Impermanence, Non-self

The basis of Buddhism is its founder's enlightened insight, considered to be nothing other than a sober perception of reality as it is. Buddhism seeks to retrieve and clarify this foundational experience, the only source of its authority.

The Buddha was born as Siddhārtha Gautama (Pali: Gotama), son of the ruler of the Śākya clan; hence he is also called Śākyamuni, "Sage of the Śākyas." Tradition gives the Buddha's dates as 560–480 BCE; but modern scholars have proposed more recent dates (463–383 according to Hajime Nakamura; 448–368 according to Heinz Bechert).[1] Everyone remembers the legend of the turning point in his life when, at the age of twenty-nine, he beheld four images of impermanence during four excursions from his father's palace: a decrepit old man, a sick man, a funeral, and a yellow-robed monk. Ancient accounts have him meditating on birth, old age, sickness, death, and pollution.[2] Behind this narrative may lie some existential crisis experienced by the youthful Gautama that anticipated his vision of human existence as marked by pain, impermanence, and non-self.

Determined to solve the painful riddle of human existence, the prince left his wife and child and sought instruction from ascetics. He spent six years in the practice of extreme austerities, which endangered his health. This path led to a dead end. Summoning all the powers of his mind, he now set himself calmly to resolve the riddle of suffering. Sitting unmoved in meditation, he repulsed the temptations of the evil Māra, lord of the world of passion, in the following words:

> I have confidence and energy and knowledge as well. So have I engaged myself in effort. . . . The body may be wasting away, but the mind gets more and more settled. More and more do mindfulness, wisdom and concentration get established in me. . . . The foremost of your armies is that of Desire [lust, *kāma*], the second is called Dislike. The third is Hunger-Thirst and the fourth is Craving. . . . One less than a hero will not be victorious over them and attain happiness. . . . I would rather die in this conflict than be alive but defeated. (*Suttanipāta* 432–40)[3]

That night, he attained supreme enlightenment, and grasped clearly the texture of human life, and the relations between this world, woven from bondage and craving, and nirvāṇa, the blissful realm of freedom.

> Thus with mind concentrated, purified, cleansed, spotless, with the defilements gone, supple, dexterous, firm, and impassible, I directed my mind to the knowledge of the destruction of the āsavas [sensual desire, desire for existence, and ignorance]. I duly realized (the truth) "this is pain," I duly realized (the truth) "this is the cause of pain," I duly realized (the truth) "this is the destruction of pain," and I duly realized (the truth): "this is the way that leads to the destruction of pain" [the Four Noble Truths]. . . . And in me emancipated arose the knowledge of my emancipation. I realized that destroyed is rebirth, the religious life has been led, done is what was to be done, there is nought (for me) beyond this world. . . . Ignorance was dispelled, knowledge arose. Darkness was dispelled, light arose.[4]

When he rejoined his five companions in asceticism, in the deer park near Benares, they were astonished at the transformation in him. He spoke to them in the following terms: "The Tathāgata, monks, is one perfected, a fully Self-awakened one. Give ear, monks, the deathless is found, I instruct, I teach *dhamma*."[5]

Speaking from a first-hand experience, the Buddha presents a teaching (Pali: dhamma; Sanskrit: dharma) which reveals the causes of suffering and the path to final escape from it.

The First Noble Truth

The Buddha expounded his dhamma in the First Sermon, with which he set the wheel of the doctrine in motion. It is centered on the Four Noble Truths. The first truth is the insight that "all this is suffering" (*dukkha*). The second truth concerns the cause of this suffering, identified as blind craving. The third truth points to the cessation of suffering, in the unconditioned state called nirvāṇa. The fourth truth teaches the way to this blissful state: the Eightfold Path of right view, right thought, right speech, right action, right livelihood, right effort, right mindfulness, and right concentration. The First Noble Truth articulates an insight fundamental to Buddhism: the realization that human life is radically unsatisfying or frustrating, a condition of dis-ease. In the earliest version it runs as follows:

> What then is the Holy Truth of Ill? Birth is ill, decay is ill, sickness is ill, death is ill. To be conjoined with what one dislikes means suffering. To be disjoined from what one likes means suffering. Not to get what one wants, also that means suffering. In short, all grasping at any of the five Skandhas involves suffering. (*Mahāvagga* I 6)[6]

No single English term can quite catch all the connotations of the word "dukkha" (*du*, bad, low; *kha*, empty, hollow). This condition of suffering and unsatisfactoriness is correlated with the fact of the impermanence of all things. Chained to the circle of birth-and-death in the world of becoming (Sanskrit: *saṃsāra*), human existence suffers from a fundamental alienation. Dukkha is a comprehensive notion, embracing physical ills such as pain, sickness, old age, and death, along with their psychical accompaniments of loneliness, anxiety, and melancholy, as well as the realities of impermanence, transitoriness, and limitation, that ineluctably mark all finite, contingent existence. ("Finite" and "contingent," are the Christian way of putting it.) Human being is analyzed into the five groups of grasping (Sanskrit: *skandha*)—corporeality, sensation, perception, volitional formations, and consciousness—each of which we grasp at desperately, identifying them with "myself," and each of which is shown to be transitory and full of dukkha.

Later generations of Buddhists seek to reproduce the existential realization of impermanence, which the Buddha attained in his enlightenment, through appropriate meditative exercises, above all the so-called *asubha-bhāvanā,* meditations on repulsive and impure things. This practice has done much to create the impression that Buddhist spirituality is morose, and one can sympathize with Friedrich Heiler when he remarks: "Our healthy Western feeling for life shudders at the gruesome images on which the Buddhist mendicant monks pondered." Yet Heiler noted that there were similar texts in Christian meditation literature.[7] Yoshinori Takeuchi, the Pure Land Buddhist philosopher of religion, finds tendencies to a "sick obsession" in the meditative analysis of "things in their origination and their transiency," i.e. decomposing bodies and the impurities of one's own body.[8]

The contemplation of rotting bodies is designed to have a shattering effect. Such images are never far from the human imagination, especially in the age of Hiroshima, the Vietnam war, and so many other horrors, though the same technology that permitted them can also numb us to them. Among the many religious figures who exploited the shock value of images of death and decay was the popular Japanese Zen abbot Ikkyū Sōjun (1394–1481) who, during the New Year festivities, used to wander through the streets of Kyoto with a skull in his hand, crying out to the revelers that this skull was truly *medetai*—a pun, since *medetai* can mean either "auspicious" or "empty eye-sockets."

It is surely a salutary thing that the realization of impermanence remain an existential matter. Neither Śākyamuni nor the Zen masters ever attempted to demonstrate in conceptual arguments this awareness of the transitoriness of things. When such demonstrations were undertaken in the Abhidharma scholasticism of early Buddhism, the existential sense of dukkha was distorted. As Takeuchi points out, to objectify the ugly and impure, what comes to be and what passes away, in a systematic classification of elements, or dharmas, in which notions such as death, old age, and suffering are handled in a dry psychological or physiological analysis, is to miss the existential thrust of the Buddha's teachings:

> In order to avoid such false interpretations, which crept in by way of Hīnayāna commentaries and strayed wide of the right path of understanding quite early on, it is necessary to recover all over again the authentic, original "existential-religious" sense of the experience of impermanency. Here I find the thought of existential philosophers and theologians most helpful for rearticulating the original spirit of primitive Buddhism for the Western intellectual world.[9]

The insight that human life is impermanent and therefore a condition of sorrow—"sad mortality"—is clearly shared by Christians also, and indeed by all human beings. The human condition, as revealed to clear-sighted analysis, is not tailored to our deepest desires, and indeed can appear as a state of alienation from what human existence ought to be. Christian reflection on this phenomenon has focused on the notion of Original Sin. Buddhist analysis pins the blame for it on desire and ignorance, two limbs of the twelvefold chain of dependent origination (*pratītya-samutpāda*), the causality behind the perpetuation of karma and transmigration. The twelve members are: (1) ignorance, (2) volitional formations, (3) consciousness, (4) mental and physical phenomena, (5) the six faculties (the five senses and mind), (6) contact, (7) sensation, (8) desire, (9) clinging, (10) becoming, (11) birth, and (12) decay and death. The causality in question is not the same thing as the efficient causality of Western philosophy. Each of the twelve members of the chain arises in dependence on what precedes it; it would not have emerged if these conditions were not present. The liberative implication of this doctrine is that what arises in dependence on conditions—the samsaric world of dukkha—can also disappear if the conditions permitting its emergence are undone.[10]

Even prescinding from the fact that several aspects of this analysis are foreign to the ontological presuppositions of the West, we may not be convinced that desire and ignorance offer a satisfactory explanation of pain and suffering. But we can hardly deny that they are major factors in the texture of human dis-ease. The Buddhist analysis chimes with the reflections of traditional Christian moralists and spiritual writers, as well as with modern existentialism. Neither Buddhism nor Christianity has produced a definitive and fully satisfying rational explanation of the mystery of iniquity underlying the phenomena of pain, impermanence, sin, and the thousand natural shocks that flesh is heir to. Keen awareness of this troubling reality impels people to seek a transformation of the unhappy state of human existence, and thus is born the religious quest for liberation or redemption. Buddhism is one of the religions that directly address this perennial human longing.

Buddhist Pessimism?

Does its basic conviction that human life is a condition of lack make Buddhism a pessimistic worldview? That conclusion has often been drawn in the West, and has caused dialogue between Buddhists and Christians to founder. It has been reinforced by a nihilistic interpretation of nirvāṇa as simple extinction. "Life is suffering" seems a sweeping declaration. The activist and optimistic West found this morose Indian doctrine unworthy of discussion. But pessimism is hardly a helpful slogan to bandy about if one wishes to bring the Buddhist doctrine into perspective. Facts are neither pessimistic nor optimistic, but true or false, and for Buddhism the truth of dukkha is a fact, established by empirical observation and logical analysis. The determination to face this fact (if such it is) is neither pessimism nor optimism, but realism—rewarded in this case by a tonic discipline. Wisdom is to see things as they are—in their "suchness" (*tathatā*).

Worldviews described as pessimistic are of three kinds: ontological, existential, and theological. Pessimistic philosophies of the first kind—nihilism or Manicheanism—declare that being as such is empty of value and meaning, that the foundations of the universe are askew. The Buddhist diagnosis does not entail anything of this sort, for it either refrains from raising questions of metaphysical ontology, or it does so only within a soteriological context, and then answers them in a way that cannot be called pessimistic. Hermann Oldenberg (1856–1920), in his classic work on the Buddha, drew attention to the silence whereby the Buddha disallowed metaphysical questions. He rejects the nihilistic interpretation of the First Noble Truth as "a strange error":

> A widespread opinion finds the core of the Buddha's doctrine in the thought that, of all that is, the true existence is the Nothing. The Nothing is alone certain. And if the world which surrounds us, or appears to surround us, is not wholly unreal, if it contains a certain, though ever so hollow a degree of existence, which cannot be ignored, this is a misfortune; and it is wrong, for right is only the Nothing. The wrong must be removed.[11]

The context makes clear that Oldenberg is speaking of philosophical nihilism, not the nothingness of mysticism. He is correcting the image of Buddhism associated with Arthur Schopenhauer (1788–1860), who spoke of "that nothingness, which as the final goal hovers behind all virtue and holiness."[12] A century later the misunderstanding he attacked is still widespread in Europe. A powerful corrective is Keiji Nishitani's (1900–1990) book *Religion and Nothingness,*[13] which clearly marks the distance between Buddhism and ontological nihilism. Only a few insignificant groups in Buddhist history appear to have asserted nihilistic theories.

The theological variety of pessimism would deny or severely limit the possibility for human beings to attain final salvation. As a path to definitive release, offered to all, Buddhism cannot be brought under this category. It is poles apart from the deep abyss of pessimism which led the Greek tragedian to declare that "never to have lived is best." The Buddhist learns from an early age to give thanks for the privilege of being born as a human, for this birth gives him the chance to hear the Buddha's teaching and to attain final liberation. Despite the great variety of the Buddhist schools they all retain the common character of being a path to liberation.

As to existential pessimism, the suspicion that the Buddhist simply got the facts of human existence wrong is not one we can comfortably indulge. The teaching is backed with the authority of a long tradition of spiritual experience. When one's eyelash is stuck in one's eye, it is painful; whereas one doesn't feel it at all on the palm of one's hand. Likewise the spiritually insightful person senses keenly the dis-ease of human existence, whereas the spiritually insensitive person may avoid noticing it. The vivid portrayals of the miseries of human life in Indian Buddhism cannot be written off as a reflection of harsh living conditions. The core of the analysis is unanswerable, as it focuses on the grim necessities that emerge concretely in every human life. A monk consoled a king, on the death of his consort, by reminding him that human existence is consigned to impermanence: it cannot be that what belongs to old age will not age, that what belongs to sickness will not fall ill, that what belongs to death will not die, that what belongs to impermanence will not pass away.

Belief in rebirth, far from alleviating the pain of impermanence, actually sharpens it, for it opens the heart-rending prospect of having to face again and again, through numerous existences, "the death of one's mother, the death of one's father, the death of one's brother, the death of one's sister, the death of one's son, the death of one's daughter, the loss of relatives, the loss of goods." But these words of the Buddha do not alter the fact that the final goal remains total liberation. Indeed the Buddhist path infallibly leads to escape from the wheel of rebirth.

The experience of pain and impermanence remained basic in Chinese and Japanese Buddhism, though in Japan the insight into impermanence is often transformed into an aesthetic attitude. The Japanese term *mujō kan* captures this shift of emphasis, for, depending on the character used for *kan,* it can mean "contemplation of impermanence," an active attitude, even a method of meditation, or "feeling of impermanence," a more passive mood. Insightful meditation on the transitory world of becoming is certainly a matter of religious significance for the earnest Japanese Buddhist, but beyond this, a keen feeling of impermanence pervades the common Japanese sense of life, and is ubiquitous in Japanese art and literature.

Turning to Christianity, we find that its account of human existence is also quite grim, if not as radical as the Buddhist one. Following Scripture, Christians view with concern the condition of humanity, not only as regards the wars or injustices that plague it at any given time, but in its basic features such as sinfulness and mortality. The *Book of Qohelet* in the Hebrew scriptures accentuates human impermanence in an almost Buddhist way, and in the New Testament, too, the *Epistle to the Romans* begins with a comprehensive portrayal of the human condition as one of need and distress. Paul's focus is on sin as the source of suffering, but he also evokes the pain of subordination to impermanence. The themes of suffering, impermanence, and death pervade Christian literature in its entirety. This insight common to East and West is reflected in a shared image of two mice, one white and the other black, which gnaw by day and by night the threads of human life. A Buddhist sūtra is the probable source of this allegory, which was transmitted to the West with the legend of Barlaam and Josaphat, thus finding its way into Christian ascetical literature. And just as the Buddha legend returned to Asia when the story of Barlaam and Josaphat was told there, so did the two mice, in sixteenth-century works of edification which were translated into Japanese. Allegorical presentations of time's corrosion—Kronos who devours his children—occur in religious literature everywhere. Here Buddhists and Christians stand on the same ground and can undertake a useful discussion on the ways in which, and also the degree to which, human existence is to be negatively viewed.

Yet however dark the picture that emerges, this is never the last word in a religion which is entirely directed to salvation or liberation. Buddhism indeed begins from a stark negative constatation of being trapped in the round of painful, impermanent existence, but this does not lead one to sink into nihilistic despair. The sober and negative formulation of the four truths may make it difficult for Westerners to perceive the light that glimmers through them. If they recall that the Buddha's sole desire in teaching the truths of dukkha, its origin, and its cessation was to show people the way to liberation, they will more readily grasp that these truths map out a horizon of hope, an advent-like human expectation—the confidence that pain can and will be overcome. This is what gives the religious teacher the ability to enunciate the First Noble Truth with such shattering and relentless insistence, just as confidence in Christ's justification of the sinner allows Paul to develop in all their terrors the themes of sin, death, judgment, and the inability of human righteousness to stand before the wrath of a righteous God. Both moments, the state of misery and the possibility of salvation, are inseparable within the religious vision. They are connected not as cause and effect, before and after, but as the poles of the religious understanding of existence.

Non-Self in the Pali Canon

An even greater obstacle to Christian-Buddhist understanding than the stereotype of Buddhism as a pessimistic worldview is the belief that Buddhism totally denies the reality of the human self. At the root of this misunderstanding we find a one-sided understanding of nirvāṇa.

Some contemporary scholars put forward a steeply reductive account of nirvāṇa as a completely negative event, simply the end of transmigration and its associated suffering. Any positive statements that would connect it with permanence or bliss are ruled out of court.[14]

Others see nirvāṇa as simply an event of ethical liberation, the end of greed, hatred, and confusion, with no transcendent or ontological implications.[15] Such reductive interpretations cannot explain the language in which nirvāṇa is evoked in radiant images of bliss, peace, security, and freedom. The literal meaning of the word "nirvāṇa" is "extinction," but this can give a misleading impression. When the Buddha was asked about the state of the Perfected One after death, he pointed out that even in this life his state is "deep, immeasurable, unfathomable as is the great ocean."[16] When a fire is quenched, one does not ask in what direction it has gone, east, west, north, or south. This is not because the fire no longer exists, but because, as an Indian audience would have gathered, the fire has returned to a non-manifested state as latent heat. Likewise, the nirvanic state is beyond our grasp, but it is not nothingness:

> "It is like a flame struck by a sudden gust of wind," said the Buddha. "In a flash it has gone out and nothing more can be known about it. It is the same with a wise man freed from mental existence: in a flash he has gone out and nothing more can be known about him. . . . When a person has gone out, then there is nothing by which you can measure him. That by which he can be talked about is no longer there for him; you cannot say that he does not exist. When all ways of being, all phenomena are removed, then all ways of description have also been removed." (*Suttanipāta* 1074, 1076)[17]

Surely this text shows that early Buddhism recognizes a distinction between the delusory empirical ego, on the one hand, and the ultimate, nirvanic state of what we may call the "true self," on the other. We shall return to this.

We have seen that when it is grasped as an existential insight the Buddhist truth of dukkha opens up a deep vision of human life, whereas if it is handled in a rationalizing style it positively blocks access to such depth of vision. This is even more the case for the doctrine of non-self (Pali: *anattā*), which is often developed in connection with the

First Noble Truth. "According to the teaching of the Buddha, the idea of self is an imaginary, false belief which has no corresponding reality, and it produces harmful thoughts of 'me' and 'mine,' selfish desire, craving, attachment, hatred, ill-will, conceit, pride, egoism, and other defilements, impurities and problems."[18] This denial of the individual self seems to put Buddhism in clear opposition to Christianity. However, when we look more closely at what is meant by non-self, this opposition is softened. Drawing again on the distinction between intellectual doctrine and lived experience, we come to recognize in the *anattā* teaching an existential insight.

One might attempt to reinforce this differentiation of the intellectual and the existential by inquiring into the relation between primitive Buddhism and later Buddhist philosophy. The teaching of Śākyamuni and his immediate disciples, that is, the earliest Buddhist preaching, was transmitted only orally until the first century BCE, when it was first fixed in writing in the Pali Canon. This is a voluminous collection of varying historical worth, and scholars distinguish between earlier and later layers. Following the example of critical scholarship of the New Testament, they have sought to isolate the earliest components of the tradition, but in the present state of knowledge this quest for the primitive form of Buddhism is extremely hazardous. What is identified as the earliest layer often depends on the scholar's presuppositions about what the Buddha could and could not have said, so it is not surprising that scholars come up with different reconstructions of the original teaching.

The First Sermon, which expounds the Four Noble Truths and the Eightfold Path, is the material that can be most securely identified as coming from the Buddha. This doesn't mean that the rest of the Pali Canon is dubious, but only that there are many irresoluble questions about its dating and originality. Most researchers tend to put a late date on abstract, theoretical passages. If one takes this approach, Buddhism is seen as emerging in ancient India as a movement of religious enthusiasm, rooted in experience. The first Buddhists were so caught up in their spiritual effort that they paid no heed to conceptual doctrinal formations.

The Pali Canon contains philosophical elements which cannot be sifted out of the text as a whole, and these elements provide rich support for the doctrinal systems of later Buddhism. In the first centuries of the growth of Buddhism, there arose the two representative schools of the Sarvāstivādins and the Theravādins, both of whom possess an Abhidharma—a collection of systematic theoretical treatises (Sanskrit: *śāstra*), forming the third of the Three Baskets (Sanskrit: *tripiṭaka*) along with the sūtras (teachings of the Buddha) and the vinaya (monastic regulations). In the philosophy of these schools the doctrine of non-self is formulated in concepts.

The First Noble Truth, in its generally accepted form (*Mahāvagga* I 6, quoted above), ends with a reference to the five skandhas—the five groups of grasping or the five aggregates: "In short, the five groups of grasping are dukkha." It is not quite certain whether this sentence occurred in the earliest version of the sermon. Oldenberg dismissed as baseless C.F. Koeppen's view that it was "a metaphysical postscript,"[19] but in two sutras found at Turfan the Four Truths are named without reference to the five skandhas.[20]

In the discourse on non-self (*Anattā-sutta*) that follows the First Sermon, the Buddha teaches that in the five groups of grasping no "I" is to be found. As Peter Harvey explains:

> In the Buddha's day, the spiritual quest was largely seen as the search for identifying and liberating a person's true self (Sanskrit: *ātman;* Pali: *atta*). Such an entity was postulated as a person's permanent inner nature, the source of true happiness and the autonomous "inner controller" of action. In Brahmanism, this ātman was seen as a universal Self identical with Brahman, while in Jainism, for example, it was seen as the individual "life principle" (*jiva*). The Buddha argued that anything subject to change, anything not autonomous and totally controllable by its own wishes, anything subject to the disharmony of suffering, could not be such a perfect true self. Moreover, to take anything which was not such a self as if it were one, is to lay the basis for much suffering.[21]

Conversely, to see that the five skandhas are not one's self, and to free oneself from concern with them, is to find freedom from anxious craving. As the conclusion of the discourse on non-self puts it:

> Disregarding the five skandhas, the disciple is dispassionate; through dispassion he is freed; in freedom the knowledge comes to be: "I am freed," and he knows: Destroyed is birth, lived is the Brahma-faring, done is what was to be done, there is no more of being such or such.[22]

The discourse insists that the self, which Indian thought postulated as constant and removed from pain, is nowhere to be found in the world of becoming, the world of the skandhas. Yet it would be hasty to assume that the idea of a true self is completely abolished. Both the First Sermon and the discourse on non-self remain silent about the ultimate reality of selfhood, and about the question as to whether the true self exists or does not exist.

Such a straightforward denial of selfhood is, however, expressed in later texts, of which the best known is the *Questions of King Milinda,* an account of the conversations of the Greek king Menander (who lived about 100 BCE) and the Buddhist monk Nāgasena. In Nāgasena's view, the self that cannot be found in the five skandhas has no existence at all. He illustrates this claim with the analogy of a chariot:

> Chariot is a mere empty sound. . . . It is on account of its having all these things—the pole, and the axle, and the wheels, and the framework, the ropes, the yoke, the spokes, and the goad—that it comes under the generally understood term, the designation in common use of "chariot". . . . Even so is it on account of all those things you questioned me about—the thirty-two kinds of organic matter in a human body, the five constituent elements of being—that I come under the generally understood term, the designation in common use, of "Nāgasena." For it was said, Sire, by our Sister Vajirā in the presence of the Blessed One: "Just as it is by the common precedent of the co-existence of its various parts that the

> word 'chariot' is used, just so is it when the skandhas are there we talk of a 'being.'"[23]

This text is influenced by the philosophy of the early Buddhist schools, which made the denial of the self the cornerstone of its system. The Sarvāstavādins developed the so-called dharma theory, according to which all that exists, from moment to moment, are the dharmas or factors of existence, which are without substance or duration. Vasubandhu's *Abhidharmakośa* (ca. 400 CE), the philosophical summa of this doctrine, enumerates seventy-five dharmas, ordered in categories. They comprise physical and psychical elements and functions of every kind, bearing no resemblance to the Aristotelian schema of substance and accidents so familiar to the West. The enumeration is an unfolding of the five skandhas, the first pluralistic formula in Buddhism. No ego is to be found among the factors of existence; rather the individual ego consists of an accumulation of factors of existence, which is nominalistically labelled the self. This dharma theory acquired great significance in the early scholastic mappings of the Buddhist path. When the Russian scholars Theodor Stcherbatsky (1866–1942) and Otto Rosenberg brought the pluralistic dharma theory to the attention of Western research,[24] and when the Belgian Louis de la Vallée Poussin (1869–1938) translated the monumental *Abhidharmakośa* in six volumes, some Western scholars saw in it the philosophical foundation on which all Buddhism rests, a questionable view which is no longer predominant. The rewarding studies of Mahāyāna have opened up in recent years a wider vista.

The dharma theory represents a one-sided interpretation of the Buddha's teaching. Takeuchi, in line with his general view that Buddhism quickly imposed a distorting objectification on its founder's message, rejects the teaching that

> The ego is nothing more than the sum total of bodily form (*rūpa*), feelings (*vedanā*), perception (*saṃjñā*), volitional impulses (*saṃskāra*), and consciousness (*vijñāna*), so that there is left no subject

> that can be called an ego. In my view Mrs. Rhys Davids is entirely correct in rejecting the propriety of the simile of the wheel, according to which the self is like a wheel, which, once dismantled, is no more than a heap of wood, since there is no wheel to begin with, any more than a self exists except as a mere name. This simile, which is frequently cited, does not in fact originate from the sayings of Gotama the Buddha, but from a nun called Vajirā who distorted the Buddha's teachings poetically in order to set forth her own views on the sorrows of being human.[25]

Takeuchi is writing in defense of the earliest form of Buddhism, which does not know the pluralistic dharma theory. He admits an *anattā-vāda* (non-self teaching), opposed to the ātman philosophy of the *Upanishads.* But he resists the dissolution of the ego into psychosomatic constituents or factors of existence which leave no place for a subject or self.

The eminent Buddhist scholar Hajime Nakamura, who like Takeuchi looks at primitive Buddhism from a Mahāyāna standpoint, insists that Buddhism from its beginnings distinguished between the empirical ego and the true self, though in Pali both notions are expressed by the same word. The contexts in which the word is used reveal the difference of meaning which Nakamura brings out. Nakamura differs from Takeuchi in regarding the five skandhas as part of the primitive teaching:

> Our human existence is only a composite of the five aggregates. Buddhism thus swept away the traditional concept of a substance called "soul" or "ego," which had up to that time dominated the minds of the superstitious and the intellectuals alike. . . . The Buddha clearly told us what the self is not, but he did not give any clear account of what it is. It is quite wrong to think that Buddhism holds that there is no self at all. . . . The wandering monk Vacchagotta asked whether there is an ego or not. The Buddha was silent. The monk rose from his seat and went away. Then Ananda asked the Buddha: "Wherefore, sire, has the Exalted One not given an answer to the questions put by that monk?" The Buddha said, "If I had

> answered: 'The ego is,' then that would have confirmed the doctrine of those who believe in permanence. If I had answered: 'The ego is not,' than that would have confirmed the doctrine of those who believe in annihilation. . . ." From the silence of the Buddha on the question of the "soul," Nāgasena, the Buddhist philosopher, drew the negative inference that there was no soul. This opinion became the orthodox teaching of Hīnayāna Buddhism.[26]

Nakamura believes that the "true self" was a concern even of primitive Buddhism. The empirical self of everyday life is tied to the world of becoming, and subject to inconstancy and pain, whereas the true, spiritual self is the subject of responsible moral and religious action. No substantiality is to be attributed to the self, nor does the Buddhist doctrine know the self as a person. The true self of Buddhism is quite distinct from that of the *Upanishads* or the Vedānta philosophy, the latter being a metaphysical entity, whereas the former is more a practical postulate, the active subject of *śīla,* morality. Both Nakamura and Takeuchi connect the true self with the attainment of liberation and nirvāṇa.

The views of these Mahāyāna writers are confirmed by Joaquín Peréz-Remón, whose thorough study of the sources leads him to these conclusions:

> Nowhere is the reality of the self absolutely and explicitly denied. . . .
>
> The anattā doctrine. . . . does not say simply that the self has no reality at all, but that certain things, with which the unlearned man identifies himself, are not the self. . . . This kind of anattā . . . . instead of nullifying the *attā* doctrine complements it. . . . The nature of the true self is never made the subject of discussion. We are only told what is not the self and consequently what the self is not. Beyond that the only thing we are told is that the self is transcendent and therefore ineffable, beyond our powers of comprehension.[27]

Edward Conze (1904–79), in the course of a highly nuanced discussion, states that: "The Buddha never taught that the self "is not," but only that "it cannot be apprehended.'"[28] However, he warns against those who "dream up a 'true Self' which, they say, will be realized by the extinction of the false, empirical self."[29] Yet he again qualifies this a little further on:

> It was clearly a mistake of lesser minds to deny categorically that the self exists. . . . One must distinguish between a *specific* negation, stating that the self cannot be identified with a clearly defined range of items, such as the skandhas, and a *general* negation, which says that "the self does not exist anywhere". . . . The non-apprehension of a self—essential to a religious life on Buddhist lines—is greatly cheapened when it is turned into a philosophical statement proclaiming that the self does not exist.[30]

Modern Theravāda Buddhism adopts no single clear stance towards the question of non-self and selfhood, and the complicated development of the Abhidharma philosophies impedes an unambiguous formulation. One finds both the denial of any kind of self, and the acceptance of a self. The position attributed to the Buddha himself rejects both nihilism (*uccheda-diṭṭhi*) and substantialism (*sassata-diṭṭhi*). The radical deniers of any kind of self can with difficulty avoid being found in a nihilistic position in the end, while the acceptance of a self leads easily to a substantialist metaphysics of being. The Buddha avoids both by his silence.[31]

A Note on Karma and Rebirth

It was probably the Buddha himself who included the ancient Indian conceptions of rebirth and karma in his teaching. They play a significant role in all forms of Buddhism. Following the ancient Indian conviction, he saw all sentient beings that exist, driven by ignorance and desire in this samsaric world, as subject to the cycle of rebirth. Their state of existence, in whatever realm, is marked by dukkha, due to its transitoriness. As a consequence of this connection between the idea of the cycle of rebirths and the First Noble Truth, in the Buddhist writings the liberation from pain is often portrayed as escape from the cycle of rebirth. Now, escape is effected through the destruction or extinguishing of desire, and desire is inextricably linked to our clinging to the identity of the empirical ego. Thus a connection with the non-self doctrine emerges. Without suppression of the greedy, anxious clinging to ego, there can be no liberation from the cycle of rebirth, which stands under the relentless law of karma, namely the repayment of all deeds accomplished in this world of becoming.

But the connection of karma and rebirth with the non-self teaching creates a logical difficulty, since the latter denies the continual existence of any empirical self, while the continuation of rebirth and the operation of karma seem to require such a self. The distinction beween the empirical and the true self is of no help here, for the true self is what is fully attained in nirvāṇa, and cannot provide the basis for rebirth. Otherwise there seems room only for the five skandhas, which are non-self, and thus incapable of providing the identifiable subject of successive existences. In the Buddhist literature the question is raised again and again as to what it is that is reborn, since there is no self in the five groups of grasping. Equally persistent is the other question, as to how the karmic retribution, according to which good deeds produce good karma and bad deeds bad karma, can be carried out without some bearer as subject. The various solutions that were proposed often showed great ingenuity.

In assessing the conceptions of rebirth and karma, it should be noted that, in their origin, these are not specifically Buddhist notions, but belong to the ancient Indian pre-Buddhist spiritual culture, and that the principal channel of their dissemination has been popular folk religiosity. In the Buddhist-inspired literature of almost every Asian country, much space is given to tales of complicated karmic retribution and marvelous rebirths. These notions have become a target of the modernizing movements in Buddhism today (more in Mahāyāna than in Theravāda). Japanese proponents of this demythologizing trend question the notion of rebirth in six (or five) realms—heavenly beings (*deva*), humans, demons (*asura,* often omitted), spirits (*preta*), animals, hells—and look instead for a new interpretation of the idea of karma.

The twelve-membered chain of dependent origination sets forth the causal links which structure the world of becoming and govern all phenomena. The most important members are the first, ignorance (Sanskrit: *avidyā*) and, in the middle group, desire or "thirst" (*tṛṣnā*). The first member, like all the others, is part of a chain that extends endlessly backward and forward, and is not to be thought of as a first cause. Questions about first and last causes are metaphysical ones, to which the Buddha replies with silence. But the twelvefold chain impresses on one's mind that nothing in the world of becoming arises by chance.

The "Great Self" in Mahāyāna

Mahāyāna retains the non-self doctrine, though with considerable restrictions, while at the same time developing the idea of the self in a way unacceptable to Theravāda, identifying the self with the universe and with the cosmic body of the Buddha. The Mahāyāna notion of the "Great Self" announces a metaphysical way of thinking that is foreign to the historical Buddha. One feature of the non-self doctrine that is given prominence in Mahāyāna is the idea that nothing has any independent existence—the self, like everything else, exists only in dependent interrelationship with all other things. Mahayanists, many modern scholars included, focus on the twelvefold chain less with regard to the wheel of rebirth, conditioned by ignorance and craving, than as an insight into the mutual interdependence of all phenomena in the world of becoming. The self, caught up in this universal relationality, extends beyond the empirical ego to the dimensions of the cosmos. Enlightenment is described as a realization of the unity between one's self and the entire cosmos: seeking one's true self, one discovers that one's "original face" is nothing other than the cosmic Buddha body (Sanskrit: *dharmakāya*).[32]

The "Great Self" is strongly brought to the fore in Zen Buddhism,* particularly in the interpretation of the experience of enlightenment (Japanese: *satori*). The modern Korean Zen master Kusan Sunim (1908–83) explains that the aim of practice is to realize that

> this world, mankind and all the animals are no different from oneself. This is precisely the "Great Self." . . . And as we know that it is not possible to separate any component from the rest of the world, both objects and the relative self cannot really exist. Therefore, the "Great Self" is precisely "no-self."[33]

Interpreted thus, the sense of being one with the cosmos is an acceptance of one's relative place in the total web of things.

In Chinese Zen texts the notion of nature or self-nature is interchangeable with that of self. For the Sixth Patriarch Hui-neng (638–713), and for his disciples, who were the original Zen masters of the T'ang dynasty, enlightenment is "looking at one's nature" (Japanese: *kenshō*). Mahāyāna philosophy and the widespread Asian belief in a correspondence between microcosm and macrocosm permit this nondual identification with reality, enjoyed only when the imprisoning illusion of the empirical ego has been shattered. Enlightenment, or satori, is a breakthrough to the true self. Hugo M. Enomiya-Lasalle describes it as

> a transrational and immediate perception of self in connection with the nondifferentiated view of all created being—giving the impression of perfect unity, grasping the authentic self of one's personality upon dissolution of the empiric ego, and coming into contact with the absolute insofar as it is the source of created being. It is an experience that allows for many variations in intensity and constitution, according to the disposition of the individual;

---

*"Zen" is the Japanese pronunciation of the Chinese "Ch'an," which is a translation of the Sanskrit term *dhyāna,* or "meditation," "concentration." For the sake of convenience, and because it has the widest currency in English, I will use "Zen" throughout this text to refer to Chinese, Korean, and Japanese teachings, masters, practices, and writings of the dhyana-Ch'an-Zen lineage.

> but which is invariably accompanied with joy, peace, certainty, and liberation from fear and doubt.[34]

In Buddhism, the true self is a theme that eludes our conceptual grasp and prompts recourse to suggestive images and paradoxes. This is to be expected, given the elusiveness of the true self in the Buddha's own teaching. Zen speaks of "one's original face before birth," "the common person of no rank," or simply "the original person." It uses cryptic symbols to point to this reality, as in the set of ten pictures of a peasant seeking and finding an ox, which he finally brings home; then, having attained the experience of unity, the peasant is seen moving in the busy market, enjoying enlightenment in the everyday.

Affinities with Christian Experiences of Selfhood

The distinction between empirical ego and true self is also found in Christian religious experience. The superficial, inconstant, ever-changing ego is contrasted with the depths of the soul, which touch the eternal. There is a tendency to associate the superficial ego with the body and the senses. Such a soul-body dualism, influenced by Greek intellectualism, is felt to be unsatisfactory, as Christians look for deeper insights into the reality of embodiment. This takes them back to the experiential level at which the distinction between superficial ego and deep self first arose.

Christian mysticism also knows a transrational, intuitive self-knowledge, though it is usually expounded in conceptual, reflexive terms. Saint Augustine, for example, writes:

> By the Platonic books I was admonished to return into myself. With you as my guide I entered into my innermost citadel, and was given power to do so because you had become my helper. I entered and with my soul's eye, such as it was, saw above that same eye of my soul the immutable light higher than my mind—not the light of every day . . . but a different thing, utterly different from all our kinds of light. It transcended my mind, not in the way

> that oil floats on water, nor as heaven is above earth. It was superior because it made me, and I was inferior because I was made by it. The person who knows the truth knows it, and he who knows it knows eternity.[35]

The encounter with self here immediately opens up on an encounter with the God who is utterly other and who is the creator of the finite self. The Buddhist intuition of self does not work in this way, but opens onto a Great Self.

Self-knowledge is linked to a contact with the ultimately real. The ecstatic enlightenment recalled by Augustine brought in its wake a vision of cosmic harmony and of the very texture of being. Thomas Merton speaks of "a kind of natural ecstasy in which our own being recognizes in itself a transcendental kinship with every other being that exists and, as it were, flows out of itself to possess all being and returns to itself to find all being in itself."[36] At this depth, self-knowledge is a matter of existential liberation, a breakthrough to spiritual freedom. The affinities between Buddhist and Christian testimonies at this existential level are striking, in spite of the divergences at the level of ontological explication.

The Buddhist, as we have seen, reaches beyond the empirical ego to the true self, attained in a breakthrough entailing a turn-about in one's normal ego-consciousness. To emerge from inauthentic existence, human beings must undergo this radical reorientation, called in Zen the "Great Death." A Chinese master asked "How is it that one who has died the Great Death is now, on the contrary, living?" Wilhelm Gundert comments as follows:

> Even the superficial reader will grasp that only one thing is in question, the Great Death which everyone must undergo once, in order to attain life and freedom. A skeptic will find the expression exaggerated, and coolly remark that here no one is actually dying. But when all that a human being is and has falls to pieces one day—an experience not confined to Buddhists—only the language of death seems adequate to describe what has occurred. . . .

> Despite the effort of some to build unscalable walls between Buddhism and Christianity, may we not ask who has found the broader way to true Christianity, those who have died the Great Death in the sense of Zen master Chao-chou [778–898], or Christians to whom such words are an empty noise?[37]

In fact Zen Buddhists gladly bring this theme into their discussion with Christians, for it is here that they believe themselves to be closest to Christianity, feeling keenly the attraction of Christ's words about "losing one's life in order to win it" or the Pauline *kerygma* of "dying in order to live." What they hear in such biblical texts as "It is no longer I who live, but Christ who lives in me" (Galatians 2.20) is the imperative of dying to this phenomenal, provisional ego, in order to attain the true self. Teilhard de Chardin (1881–1955) has powerfully actualized this Pauline idea in cosmic terms, showing that the themes of turning about, breakthrough, letting go, renunciation, and dying into life, which find their highest expression in the paschal mystery, connect with the whole reach of the human quest for self-actualization and authentic humanity, a quest inevitably entailing radical self-denial. The perfection of the cosmos, Teilhard insists, comes about only through a "death," a "night," and a decentering of one's worldly existence.

Summary

The teaching about non-self and the true self is one of the most difficult aspects of Buddhism, and one can scarcely reconstruct from the Buddhist texts an account of it entirely free from contradictions. However, we have fixed some benchmarks for a demystified grasp of the issues:

We possess no clear, unambiguous utterance of the Buddha in which he denies the true self.

Early Buddhist teaching knows no metaphysics; it rests on experience. It is in this context that we must evaluate the fact that the historical Buddha accepts no substances or souls. On this point his teaching is explicitly opposed to the ātman philosophy of the *Upanishads* and the Vedānta school.

In what are probably the earliest teachings of non-self in the texts of the Pali Canon, especially the final sentence of the First Noble Truth and the *Anattā-sutta,* we have to do not with theses of philosophical anthropology but with the involvement of the self in the experience of the radical painfulness and impermanence of human existence. The five skandhas are full of pain, since they are the object of desire and craving which falsely identify them as "self" and pursue them with blind energy. It is these painful and impermanent objects of delusive grasping that are unmasked as "not-I."

In early Buddhism there is a distinction between the empirical ego and the self as subject of human activity and of morality.

The analytical non-self teaching was developed at a later time in connection with the pluralistic dharma theory, and belongs today to the recognized doctrines of Theravāda Buddhism.

The schools of Mahāyāna Buddhism interpret the self in a thoroughly cosmic sense. In Zen, enlightenment is seen as an experience of self.

The true self, as my act of existence, is trans-categorical, not graspable in concepts, ineffable. To actualize the true self, one must undergo a dying of one's ego. Such an experience of self is an experience of transcendence, an opening to absolute reality, though the transcendence is represented in an impersonal, cosmological language rather than a personal, theological one. We shall return to these themes of transcendence and personhood in our final chapters.

III

Knowledge and Faith on the Way of Salvation

Knowledge and faith are key elements of the Buddhist way of salvation. The Buddhist conceptions of these terms are quite different from those current in the West, and their precise contours are not easily grasped by Westerners. Buddhism is concerned with concrete methods for attaining salvation. It gives precedence to knowledge over faith as the ultimately decisive factor, but at the level of practical religion faith retains a major role.

Buddhist Gnosis

In ancient India three salvific paths were distinguished: the paths of loving abandon (*bhakti-mārga*), ritual action (*karma-mārga*), and knowledge (*jñāna-mārga*). Applying this convenient division to Buddhism, we find that it comes under the third heading, which does not of course imply the total absence of the other two paths. Readers of the Pali Canon are struck by the lack of any exalted religious diction, and the prevalence of a steady analytical rationality. Indeed the entire tradition is pervaded by such rationality, which is one of the defining traits of the Buddhist spiritual attitude. Though this trait recedes as the distance from the Indian matrix increases, it never completely vanishes, and underlies even the dizzying paradoxes of Zen. The cognitive dimension of the religious effort has been accorded great weight wherever Buddhism has spread. Thus is it not surprising that Chinese and Japanese Buddhism are distinguished by great philosophical achievements, which have found their place in the cultural heritage of these peoples.

In the teaching which is regarded as the original doctrine of Śākyamuni, it is ignorance that sets in motion the twelvefold chain of dependent origination and the cycle of rebirths, and it is through knowledge that the final definitive liberation is attained. If ignorance, in tandem with desire, is the force that binds us to the wheel of painful rebirth, then the knowledge which counters this factor of perdition must have a normative significance for the path of liberation. The basic content of this liberating knowledge is the Four Noble Truths. When one hears this teaching one is set on the path to salvation, and this insight is deepened and stengthened by the disciple in the solitude of a severe monastic life. The saint (Sanskrit: *arhat*) who has mastered the ascetic path is able to root out, along with the defilements arising from worldly desires and attachments, the illusion of the empirical self and all ignorance. As Conze puts it:

> By his Gnosis he had torn the "eggshell of ignorance." He had attained Gnosis, the "super-knowledges" [the heavenly eye; the heavenly ear; the cognition of others' thoughts; the ability to recollect former lives; wonder-working powers; the knowledge that his "outflows" are dried up] and the "Powers of Analytical Insight" (*Avadāna-sataka* II 348).[1]

In this knowledge humans come to grasp not only their radically painful state of being, as well as its cause, but also the transitoriness of the world and of all things. Liberating knowledge includes awareness of one's own earlier modes of existence, and of the cycle of living things in the six realms. In the analytical, pluralistic philosophy of the Abhidharma, this knowledge is described as a discrimanitive, rational cognition. But this logical lucidity always remains at the service of liberative insight.

A religion in which knowledge is so central could well be described as gnostic in a broad sense. The religious movement known as Gnosticism emerged in the first century and expanded in the Middle East with great vitality over the next two centuries. Edward Conze and other experts on Buddhism have claimed that this movement, which arose in dependence on and in contradiction to Judaism and Christianity in the Hellenistic world, shows a strong Buddhist influence. An influence of Gnosticism on the Buddhist scriptures, on the other hand, is ruled out by chronological factors. The statements of the Pali Canon about knowledge reach back to the time of primitive Buddhism, and the earliest Mahāyāna texts precede the rise of Gnosticism. But as the movement spread east it often came into contact with Buddhism, especially in Central Asia where the Gnostic vision was represented in the powerfully effective form of Manicheanism (founded by Mani in the third century). It remains an open question to what extent these interactions affected the mainstream of each religion.

The obscurity of the historical encounter between Buddhism and Gnosticism does not exclude similarities and partial correspondences between the two, or what historians of religion call "convergences." These are the product of mental tendencies common to both, notably the tendency to give a liberating and redeeming function to knowledge. The concept of gnosis has a wider range of reference than its usage in connection with the Gnostic movement, allowing us to speak of Buddhist gnosis, Christian gnosis, and perhaps other forms of gnosis, meaning in each case the cognitive element in the salvific path. In the religious context, the simple concept of knowing or cognition takes on a redemptive hue. The term "Buddhist gnosis" characterizes the religion as centered in the cultivation of liberating cognition. For Buddhists and Gnostics alike, knowledge leads to salvation, or rather, already contains this salvation. Salvation is latent in the self and knowledge brings it to light. Moreover, human beings can find in themselves the ultimate, all-embracing reality, the All. "He who knows himself, knows the All," states one Gnostic text, and another, the *Poimandres* in the *Corpus Hermeticum,* exhorts: "Let spiritual man know himself, then he will know that he is immortal . . . and he will know the All."[2] These accounts of the gnosis in Gnosticism seem to correspond to a large extent with the Buddhist vision: Śākyamuni, too, urged his disciples to take refuge in their own self, and in Mahāyāna the self is identified with the All.

Other convergences between Buddhism and Gnosticism are not concerned with knowledge and have various sources. The Gnostic belief in rebirth, for example, goes back to the Orphics and to Plato, in whose dialogues the term "gnosis" first occurs. The Buddhists took their notions of the cycle of rebirths from the tradition of the *Upanishads.* Parallels in the esoteric dimension of both religious systems offer rich material for comparative research.

Because of the central role it attributed to knowing, Buddhism was well prepared for its encounters with Confucian rationalism in China and with the modern Western Enlightenment. No challenge from critical reason could be traumatic for a religion based on the rational dismantling of illusions and enjoying a refined sense of the relativity and provisionality of religious representations. In all the great religions, one of the principal driving forces of the process of modernization has been the need to bring a received heritage into more rationally satisfying form. Buddhist thinkers anxious to further this process have been able to draw to a remarkable extent on doctrines from early Buddhism, above all the formula of dependent origination, as well as the later speculation on emptiness, which is logically derived from this formula. In the Theravāda countries, Buddhist scholars have made efforts to show the harmony between the modern scientific world-picture and the analytic, pluralistic Theravāda philosophy. These efforts are not merely apologetic, but stem from the conviction that the Buddhist way of liberative knowledge is based on reason. Meanwhile, some Japanese scholars have interpreted dependent origination as an insight into the texture of things that anticipates and is confirmed by the notions of complementarity and indeterminacy which have surfaced in modern physics. Certainly the Buddhist worldview seems far less remote in the age of Einstein and Bohr than at previous periods in Western thought.

The secularized rationality of modern Buddhism can, however, seem rather flat when set alongside the more lofty paths of knowing on which ancient Buddhism so confidently struck out, for instance the heroic cognitive strivings described in the Pali Canon. Yet it seems that the old and the new have the same psychic roots, which explains the strong attraction modern psychology and psychiatry have for Buddhist thinkers.

Mahāyāna Wisdom

Buddhism uses three Sanskrit terms for knowledge: *bodhi, jñāna,* and *prajñā.* Bodhi, enlightenment, is the goal of the path, and in Mahāyāna it is identified with the attainment of buddhahood. Jñāna designates cognition and knowledge in the general sense, and in many texts it is synonymous with prajñā. Prajñā is integral cognition. Its Pali form, *paññā,* is the etymological basis of the Sino-Japanese *hannya-chie,* which translates the title of the *Prajñā-pāramitā* (Perfection of Wisdom) sūtras, foundational scriptures of Mahāyāna Buddhism. Prajñā is a higher cognition, contrasted with the analytical reason denoted by vijñāna, a word connected with jñāna. These brief linguistic notes may be helpful for understanding the cognitive factors that shape the Mahāyāna salvific path.

At the center of the Great Vehicle stands the figure of the bodhisattva, literally "the being of enlightenment," who, though possessing the Buddha nature, remains in the world of saṃsāra to help erring sentient beings on the way of salvation. Mahāyāna elaborately maps the bodhisattva path, which leads to the goal of enlightenment in ten stages, to which correspond ten perfections (*pāramitā*): almsgiving, keeping the precepts, forbearance, effort, meditation, wisdom, skill in means, the bodhisattva vow, strength, and knowledge. The condition for entry on the path is the initial aspiration to enlightenment, or arousing of "the thought of enlightenment" (*bodhicitta*). The sixth stage, a high point on the path, is the integral, intuitive cognition, prajñā. In fact, originally the path ended here, so that there were only six perfections to be practiced as one fared onward in this world of becoming. The four last perfections, added later, develop the sixth stage in the supramundane realm, and they, too, come to a close with a cognition designated simply as jñāna, and interpreted as Buddha-knowledge in the sense of the wisdom sūtras. The ten stages and perfections correspond to ten levels (*bhūmi*). On the sixth level the bodhisattva's wisdom is such that he stands "face to face" with nirvāṇa; the tenth level is filled with the "cloud of the Dharma," an abundance of meditative and miraculous accomplishments. An inspiring description of the spirituality of the bodhisattva path is provided by the eighth-century Indian monk Sāntideva, in his *Entering the Path of Enlightenment.*[3]

A fuller account of the metaphysical and cosmic dimensions of Mahāyāna faith will given in chapter six. Here what we wish to stress is that it is a path of life, oriented to a goal, and that attitudes of trust and belief play a major role in this religious vision. Concretely the goal is focused in terms of enlightenment. Not all enlightenment is the highest accomplishment. Zen practice knows lesser and greater enlightenments. The ideal that always hovers before the Buddhist is the Buddha's highest, unsurpassed enlightment (*anuttarā-samyaksaṃbodhi*), the Buddha-fruit, that is characterized as a cognitive event or a noetic state by the word bodhi. This characteristic is not shared by Christianity. Christian theologians have deeply reflected, and sometimes vehemently argued, as to whether knowledge or love determines the essence of the Beatific Vision, the final goal of the redeemed. Thomas Aquinas, an incomparable defender of the dignity of knowledge, finally came to teach the primacy of love, perhaps on the basis of his own mystical experience, rejoining the thought of Saint Paul (I Corinthians 13.1–13).

The Role of Faith in Buddhism

The relation of faith to rational knowledge has been a major theme of Christian theology since the Middle Ages. The unmistakable tension between these two kinds of knowing has its basis in the diversity of their sources. In Buddhism there is no knowledge that is owed directly to faith in a revelation of suprahuman provenance. Yet the word faith (Sanskrit: *śraddhā*) is often found in Buddhist writings, and we can perceive in Buddhist teaching and practice many attitudes and enactments of believing trust which bear a resemblence to Christian forms of faith.

The Pali Canon provides some fundamental descriptions of faith. Faith, by which the disciple steps onto the path of liberation, is the secure confidence that this liberation can be attained. Without faith, these texts insist, one cannot enter into the Buddha-dharma, or teaching of the Buddha, and attain salvation. The entry on the path is compared with stepping into a stream, and the attainment of salvation is consequently seen as the crossing of the stream. Thus: "Faith is the wealth here best for man—by faith the flood is crossed" (*Suttanipāta* 182, 184).[4] The flood means the impermanent, painful realm of existence, and salvation is imaged by the crossing to the "other shore." *The Questions of King Milinda* put it as follows:

> As, sire, an earnest student of yoga, on seeing that the minds of others are freed, jumps into the fruit of stream-winning or of once-returning or of non-returning or into arahantship and practises yoga for the attainment of the unattained, the mastery of the unmastered, the realization of the unrealized—even so, sire, is aspiration the distinguishing mark of faith.[5]

Through faith one takes the first step into the stream, and it is the first condition for entering the way of salvation. Without faith one could never get started on the way at all. But one builds on this faith with other faculties of vigor, mindfulness, concentration, and wisdom, listed as a set of five in a Buddhist scripture.

Faith awakens as soon as a person turns to the path of salvation and grasps the Four Noble Truths which Śākyamuni experienced in his great enlightenment and transmitted to his disciples in many doctrinal speeches. The hearers take his word to themselves in believing trust, the first disciples directly, later generations through the mediation of the holy scriptures. In the Abhidharma of the Pali Canon, faith functions as a positive factor of existence (dhamma) on the path of liberation. In the *Abhidharmakośa,* a series of factors of existence that create good, salvific karma begins with faith, to which is attributed a cleansing function: "Faith purifies the mind." The commentary by Yaśomitra (c. 700) explains that the mind stained with passions is purified by faith as unclean water is purified by a water-purifying gem. Yogācāra Buddhism, also known as Vijñānavāda, the "Mind-Only" school of Mahāyāna Buddhism, stresses faith's function in purifying the mind. Faith is seen as kindling patience, joy, and hope. Such scriptural recommendations of faith are common to all branches of the Buddhist religion.

The Triple Refuge in Mahāyāna

At the root of all faith lies a fundamental trust that leads people to expect some ultimate fulfillment of their aspirations. Buddhist texts urge their readers to confidence and perseverance in the quest for final liberation, focusing their instinct of faith on this precise goal. For instance, a basic text in the Pali Canon puts faith in immediate connection with liberation: "By faith you shall be free and go beyond the realm of death" (*Suttanipāta* 1146).[6] This faith is closely allied with hope, the hope of attaining the blissful final goal, whether envisaged as nirvāṇa or as highest enlightenment, but its primary objects are the means that lead to this goal, namely the Buddha, the dharma (the teaching), and the *saṅgha* (the community).

A scriptural text which occurs frequently in the Pali Canon teaches the disciples to take refuge in these Three Jewels (Sanskrit: *triratna*). In one version the text runs as follows:

> When a monk gets rid of the defilement of the mind that is greed and covetousness . . . he becomes possessed of unwavering confidence in the Awakened One and thinks: "Thus indeed is he the Lord, perfected, wholly self-awakened, endowed with knowledge and right conduct, well-farer, knower of the worlds, incomparable charioteer of men to be tamed, teacher of devas and mankind, the Awakened One, the Lord." He becomes possessed of unwavering confidence in dhamma and thinks: "Dhamma is well taught by the Lord, it is self-realised, it is timeless, it is a come-and-see thing, leading onwards, to be understood individually by the wise." He becomes possessed of unwavering confidence in the Order and thinks: "The Lord's Order of disciples is . . . worthy of reverence, it is a matchless field of merit for the world."[7]

This is the strongest utterance on faith in early Buddhism. The importance of the taking refuge in the Three Jewels is underlined by its place in ritual. Buddhists of every school daily renew their discipleship by reciting the formula: "I take refuge in the Buddha. I take refuge in the Dharma. I take refuge in the Saṅgha." Many other expressions of Buddhist faith can be seen as elaborations of this triple refuge.

In Mahāyāna, there are many rich developments of the theme of faith. The treatise on *The Awakening of Faith in the Mahāyāna* teaches that there are four kinds of faith:

> The first is the faith in the *Ultimate Source.* Because of this faith a man comes to meditate with joy on the principle of suchness. The second is the faith in the numberless excellent qualities of the *Buddhas.* Because of this faith a man comes to meditate on them always, to draw near them in fellowship, to honor them, and to respect them, developing his capacity for goodness and seeking after the all-embracing knowledge. The third is the faith in the great benefits of the *Dharma.* Because of this faith a man comes constantly to remember and practice various disciplines leading to enlightenment. The fourth is the faith in the *Sangha* whose members are able to devote themselves to the practice of benefiting both themselves and others. Because of this faith a man comes to

> approach the assembly of Bodhisattvas constantly and with joy and to seek instruction from them in correct practice.[8]

This text shows the broadening of the doctrine of the Three Jewels in Mahāyāna. Other Mahāyāna texts enumerate ten degrees of faith: faith, mindfulness, effort, wisdom, concentration, non-backsliding, application of merit, protection of the Dharma, discipline, and the bodhisattva vow. Confident faith, reaching forward to the goal, is the motor of progress on the spiritual path.

Let us briefly consider each of the refuges in turn.

THE BUDDHA To a remarkable extent, Buddhist faith is characterized by a bond with the person of the Buddha. The historical Śākyamuni warned his disciples against every form of cult of the person, when, as some poignant passages in the Pali Canon show, they were all too inclined to cling to his person. Before his entry into nirvāṇa he urged them to find their support in themselves and in the teaching, the dharma. Yet the ordinary behavior of the first Buddhist communities, as portrayed in early accounts, is pervaded by an atmosphere of believing trust of the disciples in their master; boundless is their faith in his word, which shows them the path of salvation. This attitude of believing trust came to the fore very soon after Śākyamuni's departure.

> They call him Buddha, Enlightened, Awake, dissolving darkness, with total vision, and knowing the world to its ends, he has gone beyond all the states of being and becoming. He has no inner poison-drives; he is the total elimination of suffering. This man, brahmin Bāvari, I follow.
>
> It is like a bird that leaves the bushes of the scrubland and flies to the fruit trees of the forest. I too have left the bleary half-light of opinions; like a swan I have reached a great lake.
>
> Up till now, before I heard Gotama's teaching, people had always told me this: "This is how it has always been, and this is how it will always be"; only the constant refrain of tradition, a breeding ground for speculation.

> This prince, this beam of light, Gotama, was the only one who dissolved the darkness. This man Gotama is a universe of wisdom and a world of understanding, a teacher whose Dhamma is the Way Things Are, instant, immediate, and visible all around, eroding desire without harmful side-effects, with nothing else quite like it anywhere in the world. (*Suttanipāta* 1133–7)[9]

The titles bestowed on Śākyamuni in such rapturous testimonies formed the beginning of the process that elevated him to suprahuman status, a process accompanied by an ever deepening attitude of believing trust in his person. The influence of this devotion on Buddhist art will occupy us in chapter seven.

The Buddha, in Mahāyāna piety, is no longer merely the historical Śākyamuni, but the densely populated pantheon of the Buddhas of the Mahāyāna sūtras, which has sometimes created the misleading impression that Mahāyāna Buddhism is a kind of polytheism. In the theory of the three bodies of the Buddha, Śākyamuni figures as the exemplar of the lowest body, the "transformation body," while the usual objects of faith are the "reward bodies" of the glorified Buddhas dwelling in innumerable Buddha lands. The cosmic Buddha body (dharmakāya) configures the absolute in a way that recalls this exuberant faith to a focus on transcendence, as we shall see in chapter six.

THE DHARMA Faith in the dharma means faith in the word of the Buddha as set down in the scriptural canon, an external authority. The believer is a hearer of the word. This hearing is described as follows in an early text of the Pali Canon:

> One having faith draws near; he gives ear and hears Dhamma and tests the meaning of the things he has borne in mind, and they please him; mindfulness and zeal are produced in him; weighing it all up, he strives; being self-resolute he realizes the highest truth itself and sees it in all its detail by means of wisdom.[10]

As one appropriates the Buddha's word it becomes a matter of one's own insight. Moreover, all teachings are regarded as at bottom unsatisfactory and empty. One must not become attached to views. The Zen school, with no departure from orthodoxy, gives dramatic expression to this attitude in word and gesture. Doctrines are treated as time-bound and culture-bound indications of the essential matter, fingers pointing at the moon which they can never grasp. "The wise man points at the moon; the fool looks at the finger."

Buddhist faith is nourished by constant commerce with the Scriptures. There are many touching examples of reverence for the holy books in the tradition, and even today the pious copying out of a scripture is regarded as a meritorious work. Thus Nikkyō Niwano, former president of the modern popular Buddhist religion, the Risshō Kōseikai, devoted himself during eighty-three days to copying out the *Lotus Sūtra* before erecting a huge statue of the Buddha in the headquarters of his religion. The "Bible in Stone" at Kuthodaw monastery in Mandalay, Burma offers singular evidence of this reverence for the Buddha's word: on seven hundred twenty-nine stone disks, each lodged within a pagoda, the entire Pali Canon is inscribed; these small pagodas are arranged around a big one, each pagoda symbolizing the Buddha. A similar impression of the sacral character of the scripture is aroused by the oldest woodblocks of the Chinese Canon, eighty-one thousand blocks reproducing Theravāda and Mahāyāna texts, preserved in Haeinsa Monastery in Korea.

An example of a religious practice centered on the veneration of a single sūtra is the school of Nichiren (1222–82), widespread in Japan, whose chief object of faith and devotion is the *Lotus Sūtra.* This sūtra demands not only faith in its message but also veneration of the scriptural text itself. At many places it promises its devotees indescribable wealth as a reward and threatens despisers with severe punishment. The invocation of the holy name of the sūtra—*Namu Myōhōrengekyō,* or "Praise to the Lotus Sūtra of the Mystic Law" (called the *daimoku)*—is the principal form of Lotus piety, avidly practiced by the masses of the sect's followers. The quintessence of the sūtra is concentrated for believers in the written characters of its title. In the holy title is present the supratemporal Buddha who manifests himself as the essence of the universe in the sixteenth book of the sūtra (as we shall see in chapter six). The one who recites the title with faithful trust is assured of becoming a Buddha.

The dharma thus acquires an extremely wide sense in Mahāyāna Buddhism, where dharma as an ontological principle is identical with the Buddha in his cosmic, universal aspect. The dharma body of the Buddha is thought of as present in all things and identical with all things. It is the universal Buddha nature or Buddha mind, faith in which lies at the basis of the practice of meditation. Faith in the dharma remains firmly oriented to the attainment of enlightenment. For no matter how grandiose the objects of faith become, every form of faith, in Mahāyāna as in Theravāda, is correlated with a concrete practice.

THE SAṄGHA Taking refuge in the saṅgha is an essential co-condition of the other two refuges. From its beginnings, the Buddhist religion confronts us as a communal, and specifically as a monastic formation. The Buddha gathered his phalanx of disciples about him, allowed them to share in his own experience, and urged them to earnest striving after salvation. Of the early organization we know little, but that the saṅgha emerged as an established power soon after the Buddha's departure is clear from the records of the early Buddhist Councils. For generations, Buddhists were convinced that they could best work out their salvation in a communal context. The monastic organization of contemporary Theravāda countries gives an idea of what the early saṅgha was like.

Despite the organizational upheavals, community is central to Mahāyāna also. Attainment of liberation was no longer interpreted primarily in monastic terms, but Buddhists continued to work together in schools, lines of tradition, and monasteries, and this communal organization played a great role in the transmission of the decisive experiences of faith. In Mahāyāna, the saṅgha is extended to the assembly of bodhisattvas. The rich cultic life of Mahāyāna is very largely a communal one. The temple space and the meditation hall are for many Buddhists the privileged site of their religious experiences. This is true also for a Buddhism that declares its lay character and for modern Buddhist popular religions, which are indeed marked by a strong communal life. Some of these new forms of Buddhism put the emphasis on returning to primitive Buddhism, and in their recitation of the three refuges, the third refuge takes on a full, concrete content. Though Buddhism has not yet developed a theology of community, it is clear that Buddhist faith has an essential communal dimension.

The Buddhism of Faith

In a posthumous work, D.T. Suzuki (1870–1966) expounds the deep spirituality of the Amida Buddhism professed by the True School of the Pure Land (Jōdo Shinshū) in Japan.[11] It is well known that Suzuki maintained a warm sympathy for Amida piety throughout his life. I shall never forget one of his last lectures in Tokyo a few months before his death on the "Wonderful Good Men" (*myōkōnin*), a group of Japanese Amida devotees whose simplicity of life and pure goodness of heart recall the *poverello* of Saint Francis Assisi (1181–1226). Suzuki's little book appeared in German with the two fitting titles, which can be rendered into English as *Amida—the Buddha of Love* and *The Power of Inner Faith.*

This form of Buddhism deserves our special attention because of its wide dissemination in East Asia; indeed, in some periods, the majority of the inhabitants of this densely populated region were devotees of this Buddha of Love. Amitābha (Japanese: Amida), the Buddha of Immeasurable Life and Inconceivable Light, throned in his Western Paradise, the Pure Land (Sanskrit: Sukhāvati; Japanese: Jōdo), attracts countless worshipers on account of the splendor of his appearance, but it is on his promises that believers in him rely above all. These promises or vows were first made in his former life as a monk, unimaginably long ago; as a bodhisattva he had the name Dharmākara. The cult of Amida in the Pure Land school is based on the three so-called Amida sūtras, namely the *Smaller Pure Land Sūtra,* the *Larger Pure Land Sūtra,* and the *Meditation Sūtra.*[12] The second of these lists the forty-eight Original Vows (Japanese: *hongan*), including especially the eighteenth, in which the bodhisattva renounces his entry into nirvāṇa until all who call on the holy Buddha name have been reborn in the Pure Land.

Pure Land thinkers have devoted much reflection to the themes of faith and grace, developing something like a theology of faith, which reached its acme in the Japanese patriarch Shinran (1173–1263), who has an outstanding place in Japanese religious history. In Buddhist tradition, faith is an act of the human will by which one aspires to realize the ideals set before one, and previous Pure Land thinkers had presented faith and the recitation of the *nembutsu* (the invocation of the name of Amida) as meritorious acts gaining salvation. For Shinran, however, faith and merit are purely the gift of Amida Buddha, and one recites the nembutsu not in order to be saved but as an act of gratitude for salvation received. Shinran made much of this faith in the Buddha's efficacy and saving power, which he called "Other Power" (Japanese: *tariki*) in contrast to making one's own efforts to achieve salvation, or "Self Power" (Japanese: *jiriki*). Faith is the cardinal point of Shinran's doctrine; it is the cause and condition of salvation, and thanksgiving plays a great role in the Jōdo Shinshū school he founded, insofar as the virtuous moral life is seen as rooted in gratitude. His predecessors looked to salvation in the future, but Shinran held that the believer could be assured of ultimate salvation here and now. The believer dances and leaps for joy, because of this assurance, and joy pervades all his activities.

A convenient summary of Shinran's thought can be found in the posthumous *Record of Lamentations over Departures from the Teaching* (*Tannishō*) compiled by his disciple Yuien. Here Shinran celebrates the sole efficacy of the faith granted by Amida with a paradoxical verve that has prompted comparisons with Luther[13]:

> Even a good person can attain birth in the Pure Land, so it goes without saying that an evil person will. Though such is the truth, people commonly say, "Even an evil person attains birth, so naturally a good person will." This statement may seem well-founded at first, but it runs counter to the meaning of Other Power estab-

> lished through the Primal Vow. For a person who relies on the good that he does through his Self Power fails to entrust himself wholeheartedly to Other Power and therefore is not in accord with Amida's Primal Vow.[14]

Shinran summons the Buddhists of his time to faith, which alone can bring rescue to sinful humans during this Latter Days of the Law (Japanese: *mappō*), as he believed it to be. He urges them to practice the nembutsu: " 'Saved by the inconceivable working of Amida's Vow, I shall realize birth into the Pure Land': the moment you entrust yourself thus, so that the mind set upon saying the Name arises within you, you are brought to share in the benefit of being grasped by Amida, never to be abandoned."[15]

Shinran's teaching on faith was vehemently attacked by the adherents of the traditional schools of his time, who defended the "holy way" or "path of sages" (Japanese: *shōdō*) of strenuous study of the scriptures and vigorous meditation, against the simplification represented by nembutsu practice. Unperturbed, Shinran repeated his call to faith:

> At present, people of the singlehearted practice of the nembutsu and those of the Path of Sages contrive disputes over the dharma, each claiming their own way to be superior and others' inferior. . . . Without the slightest argument, one should simply reply: "When a foolish being of low capacity like myself, one unfamiliar with even a single character, entrusts himself, he is saved. Since I accept and entrust myself to the teaching, for me it is the supreme dharma, though for one of lofty powers it might seem utterly base."[16]

In his doctrinal treatise, *The True Teaching, Practice, and Realization of the Pure Land Way* (*Kyōgyōshinshō*), Shinran stresses the centrality of faith, and he celebrates it in a hymn inserted in the treatise.[17] The hymn covers the basic Pure Land ideas and places Shinran's teaching in relation to the seven patriarchs of the school. The first of the patriarchs is the great Indian thinker Nāgārjuna (second century), the originator of the Mādhyamika philosophy of the Middle Way. He is declared to have urged people to trust in the easy practice of the nembutsu and to respond with gratitude to Dharmākara's vow of great compassion. Second on Shinran's list is Vasubandhu (316–96), a major figure of the Yogācāra school of Indian Buddhist philosophy—here presented as a devotee of Amida and the Pure Land sūtras and as the author of a treatise thereon.

It is certain that devotion to Amida and invocation of his name have their roots in India, but the school first flourished in a sustained way in China under the three patriarchs T'an-luan (476–542), Tao-ch'o (562–645), and Shan-tao (613–81). They expressly preached the doctrines of the unique efficacity of Other Power and of faith as the cause of birth in the Pure Land, and they recommended the nembutsu as the sole practice, excluding all others. Shinran's hymn celebrates Shan-tao with special warmth:

> Shan-tao alone in his time clarified the Buddha's true intent;
> Sorrowing at the plight of meditative and non-meditative practicers
> and people of grave evil,
> He reveals that Amida's light and Name are the causes of birth.[18]

The sixth patriarch, Genshin (942–1017), a Japanese, is praised for "Ascertaining that minds devoted to single practice are profound, to sundry practice, shallow."[19] However, modern scholars tell us that, to the contrary, Genshin's position was that "meditation is superior and recitation is inferior."[20] The seventh patriarch, the pious Hōnen (1133–1212) was Shinran's teacher, whom he trusted unconditionally.

> Establishing in this remote land the teaching and realization that are
> the true essence of the Pure Land way,
> He transmits the selected Primal Vow to us of the defiled world.[21]

Hōnen asserted the clear superiority of the practice of nembutsu. The tradition has it that whether walking or standing, sitting or lying down, he constantly carried the name of Amida in his heart and formed it on his lips.

Hōnen also taught that the Buddha comes to meet his devotees at the moment of death, an event known as the *raigō,* which became the theme of many sublime paintings. He insisted so much on the need to keep the Buddha in mind at the moment of death, warning that one could lose the power of faith at the last moment, that this became a source of anxiety among his followers. Constant recitation of the name became a kind of insurance against the danger of missing rebirth in the Pure Land. Shinran cut this residual reliance on Self Power by making faith entirely the creation of Other Power, something firmly established in us as soon as we accept Amida Buddha as our savior.

> The nembutsu as practised by the jiriki followers puts the Buddha away from themselves far in the West, and thinking that they are worthless beings they would now and then recollect the Original Vow of the Buddha and pronounce his Name. . . . They have no definite assurance of the Pure Land. This position is like that of a feudal retainer who only occasionally comes out in the presence of his lord. His relationship with the latter can never be intimate and trustful. Such a devotee is all the time in an unsettled state of mind as to how to court the favor of the Buddha, how to be reconciled to Him, how to win his loving consideration, and this very fact of his uncertainties alienates him from Buddha, resulting in the unharmonious relationship between the devotee's unsettled mind and Buddha's great compassionate heart.[22]

Shinran, then, pushes to its last consequences the message of trust in the exclusive efficacity of Other Power. In the *Record of Lamentations* a person's own activity is completely ruled out. A genuine problem of human religiosity here comes to the fore, namely the tension between grace and freedom, between believing trust and personal effort. Luther resolved this tension with his well-known *sola fide* teaching, while the French spiritual guide Fénelon (1651–1715), basing himself on the spiritual experiences of Madame Guyon (1648–1717), invoked *l'amour pur* (pure love), which was denounced as a suspect quietism by Bossuet (1627–1704). Each of these doctrines stems from a limit situation which few would be capable of sustaining. The numerous adherents of the True Pure Land school show their founder Shinran the highest reverence, but this has not dispensed them from the struggles against moral slackness and religious laxity which are so common in the history of the school.

From a psychological point of view, there cannot be a very great difference between the attitude of faith shown in the veneration of Amida and Christian faith in God or Christ, at least at the level of popular religion. However, there is a theological point not to be overlooked. In Mahāyāna theory, the cult of a personal Buddha is merely a provisional stage, a skillful means for those who have not raised their minds to a purer grasp of the absolute. Even for Shinran, faith is "the easy way of practice to be followed by those of inferior capacity," and it is nirvanic enlightenment that is identified as the truly salvific instance. This he expects in the future life:

> When, by allowing ourselves to be carried on the ship of Amida's Vow, we have crossed the ocean of birth-and-death, so full of suffering, and attained the shore of the Pure Land, then the moon of awakening to things as they truly are will immediately appear.[23]

Faith is always a transitional attitude for the Buddhist, who is under the obligation to forge ahead towards enlightenment or nirvāṇa, a goal beyond all mediations. Can something similar be said of Christian faith? The question is certainly worth pondering. It would demand that one examine the different significance which the Founder and the community have for the believers in each tradition. The Buddha, as an object of faith, is provisional, he melts into the general texture of the Buddhist experience. This could never be said of Christ for the Christian, for whom Christ's coming is the unsurpassable fulfillment, his grace the eschatological salvation; Christ is not just the mediator of faith, but its cause, its goal, and its saving content, though any representation of Christ that one may form in this life is indeed merely provisional.[24]

A remark, finally, on the this-worldly aspects of Buddhist faith. If the ultimate liberation aimed at goes beyond the horizons of daily life, Buddhists nonetheless expect a liberating effect in the here and now, and are not afraid to express this hope in prayer and in rites directed to earthly welfare. Magical ingredients often lessen the religious worth of these exercises, without however entirely annulling it. The quest for political liberation as a religious goal, which has had such a potent impact in the Christian communities of Latin America, has also made itself felt in third world Asian countries.[25] Popular Buddhism has also brought comfort and inspiration to Japanese workers who live oppressive and monotonous lives. The vigor and variety of this pastoral outreach is evident in the flood of popular Buddhist publications, which deal with all the questions and anxieties of their readers, appealing to healthy common sense or to the trustworthy experience of the spiritual guide, but also to belief in higher powers. The Western reader may feel that the discussion never rises above sensitive advice, and that a decisive word remains unspoken. Yet often a sūtra text or the word of a patriarch will appear suddenly at the end, and the reader who brings a spirit of faith will find sustenance in it. The Buddhist New Religions of Japan combine the aspiration to return to the historical Buddha and to promote the welfare of people in daily life, for example through self-help groups which empower ordinary people to deal with their needs. As they share their spiritual or material problems they invoke the Buddha as a healer. This down-to-earth faith is far removed from the abstract pessimism which Westerners often associate with Buddhism.

Thus the basic human experience, whereby one breaks through the bounds of ego to open oneself to an all-embracing, protecting, and helping Power, works itself out in Buddhism in a distinctive style. Knowledge and nescience, transcendent faith and this-worldly confirmation, blend here in a rich variety of forms.

IV

Wisdom and Compassion

In Buddhism and Christianity, the words "wisdom" and "compassion" carry rich overtones. They cannot be separated: wisdom without compassion is empty, compassion without wisdom is blind. A focus on compassionate wisdom or wise compassion matches our modern sense of life, inasmuch as it approaches the religious question from an anthropological standpoint, that is, from the human situation. Buddhism is not a philosophy but a religion of salvation, a path of liberation. Its point of departure is the distressful situation of unsaved humanity. The role of wisdom and compassion, working together inseparably, is to help human beings in the situation of suffering which presses hard upon them.

Benevolence and Compassion in Early Buddhism

The compassion preached by the Buddha is no mere ornament of the virtuous life but is the crowning factor in the ethics of Buddhism.[1] Buddhist ethics are firmly rooted in concern for the worldly good of suffering humans, and they seek expression in concrete social and communitarian action. They include a deep sensitivity to the life of the cosmos, an ecological consciousness which combines esthetic refinement with a sense of responsibility, forbidding the manipulative use of things as mere instruments.

Buddhist compassion is not merely an ethical attitude, but is intimately connected with religious wisdom. It implies the entire path of enlightenment. Whenever the theme "Buddhism and Christianity" has come into view, in apologetical comparison, in sharp confrontation, or in an earnest quest for mutual rapprochement, interest has centered on the relation between Buddhist compassion and Christian love. Just as in the assessment of nirvāṇa, there has been considerable divergence of views in regard to this theme, which, as has quickly appeared, is also a difficult one. Though people have remarked again and again on the palpable closeness of the two ideals, it has been impossible to gloss over a sense that they remain profoundly different. The Buddhist language of compassion has sounded remote and disengaged to Western ears, and this has created another barrier to understanding.

Semantic discrepancies reveal here, as so often, a far-reaching divergence in the mentalities and emotional reflexes of Christians and Buddhists. It may be helpful, therefore, to clarify this terminological aspect. In Pali and Sanskrit there are two terms which are close in meaning but not quite synonymous: *mettā* (Sanskrit: *maitrī*) and *karunā,* both of which are used in early Buddhism. The first of these words shares the same root as *mitra,* friend, and thus literally means the disposition of friendship, or friendliness. Other suitable translations are kindness, benevolence, and generosity. Karunā is compassion in the strict sense: suffering on account of the suffering of the other and suffering with the other. In the Mahāyāna terminology of China and Japan the two terms mettā and karunā are combined in a single expression *jihi,* composed of two Chinese characters corresponding to the two terms.

In addition, Buddhism also uses the word "kāma" for sensual, erotic love or desire (similar to "tṛṣṇâ," literally thirst, which occurs in the twelvefold chain of dependent origination) and bhakti for trustful devotion. The Buddhist vocabulary is thus quite rich, but it does not possess the word "love." For Christians this word summarizes a large ensemble of forms of human feeling and willing, uniting different strands of meaning, such as the attitudes distinguished under the titles *eros, philia,* and *agape.* The subdivisions of love worked out by Plato and Aristotle were enriched and Christianized in the language of Pauline and Johannine theology and the speculations of the Church Fathers. There is simply no equivalent in Asian languages for what the word "love" means in the Western context.

Given this state of affairs, whenever we meet the word "love" in a quotation from Buddhist literature in a European language, we must ask what the original term was, as this is what determines the sense. The translation of a Buddhist text can mislead the reader, since the associations of the original word are often not made apparent. When people characterize Buddhism as teaching that love only gives rise to suffering and that suffering is removed with the removal of love and pleasure, "love" refers to kāma or tṛṣna, the desire that ties one to the wheel of rebirth. Mettā and karunā belong to a quite different sphere. Linguistic imprecision on such topics has been a source of confusion up to quite recently.

Turning now from the terminology to the substance of the doctrine, we look first to the figure of the Buddha. In the consciousness of his community as reflected in the traditions about his life, what is remembered, in immediate connection with his enlightened wisdom, is his benevolence and kindness, his unrestricted pity for all sentient beings. This pity is seen as the motivation of his preaching. In enlightened wisdom, the Buddha discovered the cause of sufferings and the way of liberation from them, and his compassion prompted him not to enjoy only for himself his liberating knowledge, but to set in motion the wheel of teaching for the salvation of all sentient beings. These motives are stressed in a biography of the Buddha composed in the second century:

> Now that he has grasped the principle of causation, and finally convinced himself of the lack of self in all that is, he roused himself again from his deep trance, and in his great compassion he surveyed the world with his Buddha-eye, intent on giving it peace. When, however, he saw on the one side the world lost in low views and confused efforts, thickly covered with the dirt of the passions, and saw on the other side the exceeding subtlety of the Dharma of emancipation, he felt inclined to take no action. But when he weighed up the significance of the pledge to enlighten all beings he had taken in the past, he became again more favorable to the idea of proclaiming the path to Peace. (Aśvaghoṣa, *Buddhacarita* 14)[2]

Just as important as the opening of his eye of wisdom at the first shining of the morning star is his rejection of the suggestion of Māra, the evil one, who urged him to enter there and then, unconcerned by the sufferings of sentient beings, into the blissful repose of nirvāṇa.

The life of the Buddha makes concretely visible the basic benevolence of his character. His nephew Devadatta, who was full of malice towards him, set a fierce elephant at him:

> The elephant rushed towards the Lord, murder in his heart, and the people wept and held up their arms. But without hesitating the Lord went on, collected and unmoved, and without any feeling of ill-will. His friendliness made him compassionate towards all that lives. . . . When the elephant had come quite near, the Sage's spiritual power soon brought him to his senses, inducing him to lower his body and place his head on the ground. . . . The Sage stroked the elephant's head, as the moon touches a cloud with its rays. (Aśvaghoṣa, *Buddhacarita* 21)[3]

This is only a charming legend, as no doubt is the story elsewhere of his gentle forgiveness of his nephew. Nonetheless, whatever their historical core, the Buddha lives through such legends, in the memory of his followers, as the highest earthly embodiment of mercy. They regard compassionate benevolence as the principal virtue for the reason that it is the virtue of the Buddha. This first concretization of Buddhist compassion, namely, the living benevolence of the Buddha himself, has a significance that is not exhausted by all subsequent systematization and analysis.

The doctrine of mettā, benevolence, occurs in connection with meditation in a text of the Pali Canon, the *Mettā-sutta* from the *Sutta-nipāta,* which has been compared with Paul's hymn to charity in 1 Corinthians 13. The text formulates the blessing wished by the benevolent person as follows: "Whatever living beings there be: feeble or strong, tall, stout or medium, short, small or large, without exception; seen or unseen, those dwelling far or near, those who are born or those who are to be born, may all beings be happy![4]" The absence of all bad will is to guarantee happiness. The text continues: "Let none deceive another, nor despise any person whatsoever in any place. / Let him not wish any harm to another out of anger or ill-will."[5] The ethical tone of these last words cannot be missed. Then the text reaches its climax: "Just as a mother would protect her only child at the risk of her life, even so, let him cultivate a boundless heart towards all beings."[6] What is called for here is a meditative action, as the following words make clear: "Let his thoughts of boundless love pervade the whole world: above, below and across without any obstruction, without any hatred, without any enmity. Whether he stands, walks, sits or lies down, as long as he is awake, he should develop this mindfulness."[7]

The exercise of awakening and radiating forth benevolence recurs frequently in the Pali Canon as a form of meditation, formalized as the meditation on the four "immeasurables" or "Brahma dwellings" (*brahmavihāra*):

> He abides, suffusing one quarter of the world with the thought of Friendliness; likewise the second, the third, the fourth quarters, above, below, around, everywhere, he abides pervading the whole world with all sentient beings, all as himself with his thought of Friendliness, far reaching, grown great, immeasurable, free from hatred, free from malice.[8]

The three other immeasurables are compassion in the strict sense (karunā), sharing in joy (*muditā*), and equanimity (*upekkhā*). These three states of mind are awakened and radiated out into the world in exactly the same way as benevolence. This meditative exercise cultivates the Buddhist sense of solidarity. It creates an escape from egocentrism, a stepping over of the self to the other, a compassion that penetrates the whole world in the four directions.

However, the value of such meditation may be variously estimated, depending on whether one considers its effects on the meditator or on human society. Western critics object that the subjective benefit to the meditator may be great without any great profit to his fellow-humans. This criticism hits the mark if the general benevolent dispositions are not matched by practical action. Less justified is the accusation, also often met with from Western critics, that Buddhist benevolence does not get beyond a negative posture. It is true that the avoidance of evil is a prevalent theme in Buddhist preaching. The *Mettā-sutta,* as we have seen, expressly urges us to put away all ill will, hate, resentment, and irritation. The Golden Rule, too, is formulated negatively in Buddhist texts, for instance in connection with the prohibition of killing:

> All are frightened of the rod.
> Of death all are afraid.
> Having made oneself the example,
> One should neither slay nor cause to slay. (*Dhammapada* 129)[9]

Buddhists are convinced that human happiness in this world can be extended only by constant, intensive effort to do away with evil attitudes, above all hate and hostility. Should we complain if they have put their finger on the causes of so much human suffering? If with their characteristic discretion they prefer to designate mettā in negative formulations, they nonetheless clearly mark out the way of positive, active benevolence.

A weightier objection is that the status of benevolence is diminished when it is fitted into the fourfold scheme of the meditation exercise. Such schemes usually show a progression from lower to higher stages, and mettā is here put at the lowest stage. The two following stages, karunā and muditā, are indeed virtues of a related kind—corresponding to the Pauline injunction, "Rejoice with those who rejoice, weep with those who weep" (Romans 12.15)—but the highest stage of upekkhā, equanimity, designates a state of feeling which is unmoved by joy and sorrow, honor and dishonor. Heiler remarks that here "an affective and helpful fraternal love is estimated only as a preliminary stage of the totally asocial ideal of salvation."[10] This is a severe judgment and needs to be qualified, but it is certain that a relativization of benevolence is implied in its insertion into the fourfold scheme. The great Sri Lankan commentator Buddhaghosa (fifth century) suggestively compared the four attitudes with a mother's feelings toward four sons: "a child, an invalid, one in the flush of youth, and one busy with his own affairs."[11]

In general, early Buddhist meditation does not provide the most important material for demonstrating mettā. There are other more convincing testimonies:

> Just as, O monks, whatever may be the light of the starry forms, all together do not equal a sixteenth part of the light of the moon, for the latter, transcending them, doth shine, and glow, and radiate; even so, O monks, whatsoever materials there may be for the acquisition of Virtue, connected with the Substrata, all these do not equal a sixteenth part the value of Friendliness, which is an emancipation of the thoughts [i.e. the state of *samādhi*]; for Friendliness, verily, an emancipation of the thoughts, transcending everything, doth shine, glow, and radiate.[12]

These words can be taken to show that friendliness or love, mettā, is the highest virtue. Here it is placed in the neighborhood of spiritual liberation, a connection that will be thought out in its implications in Mahāyāna Buddhism.

WISDOM AS THE GROUND OF COMPASSION

In the Buddhist vocabulary, wisdom figures as the highest value. Wisdom, or prajñā, is actually identified with Buddha, the Enlightened One, since wisdom and enlightenment (bodhi) designate his intrinsic nature. The reason wisdom and compassion belong together is that out of wisdom flows compassion, in the strong sense of sympathetic suffering with all sentient beings. From the Buddha, who in enlightenment has attained complete possession of wisdom, stream forth benevolence and mercy.

Wisdom and compassion are central in all forms of the Buddhist religion and all Buddhists revere the supreme wisdom of the enlightened Śākyamuni, yet wisdom is not always understood in the same way and in its full significance. The Pali word "paññā" already admits a variety of translations: cognition, insight, knowledge, and wisdom. The Eightfold Path makes no mention of wisdom, but other important early Buddhist schemas, such as the five faculties that lead to enlightenment, have wisdom as their culmination. In one Pali text wisdom is celebrated as power, sword, light, radiance, and jewel.[13] The résumé of the early Buddhist path in the formula of the Three Disciplines—morality (Pali sīla; Sanskrit: śīla), concentration (Pali and Sanskrit: samādhi), wisdom (Pali: paññā; Sanskrit: prajñā)—places wisdom above meditative concentration. This formula from the early period shapes the teaching of many Buddhist schools down to the present.

The later pluralistic dharma theory destroys every possibility of a love relationship between two persons at its root, for, as Edward Conze points out:

> There is a logical contradiction between the method of wisdom [the dharma theory], which sees no persons at all, but only dharmas, and the method of the Unlimited [the four Brahma dwellings] which cultivates relations to people as persons. The meditation on dharmas dissolves other people, as well as oneself, into a conglomeration of impersonal and instantaneous dharmas.

> It reduces our manhood into five heaps, or pieces, plus a label. If there is nothing in the world except bundles of dharmas—as cold and as impersonal as atoms—instantaneously perishing all the time, there is nothing which friendliness and compassion could work on. One cannot wish well to a dharma which is gone by the time one has come to wish it well.[14]

To be sure, the dharma theory is not "offered as a metaphysical theory of the world, to be discussed and argued about" but "as a practical method of destroying through meditation, those aspects of the commonsense world which tie down our spirit."[15] How deeply such a method is able to influence people, and whether in practice they combine notional impersonalism with practical personalism, are questions difficult to answer. It seems, in any case, that Śākyamuni keeps the space for mettā open, and the same may probably be said of later forms of Buddhism. Nothing is more common in human life than the coexistence of contradictory attitudes, and the influence of every philosophical method is a limited one.

The Mahāyāna schools may not have been any more successful than the Abhidharma in furnishing a satisfactory philosophical basis for compassion. In Mahāyāna the connection between emptiness and wisdom turns on the theme of emptiness, the perception that all things are empty (*śūnya*). This does not mean that nothing exists. Rather, through demonstrating the insubstantiality, indeterminacy, and formlessness of the phenomenal world, this philosophy opens access to transcendental reality, or to the suchness (tathatā) of what is, the unity of being, beyond and beneath the discriminations of everyday consciousness. The wisdom that has gone beyond (prajñāpāramitā) clearly grasps the nothingness of all representations and conceptual knowledge, and on the basis of this insight, realized in enlightenment, all aspects of human life undergo a radical relativization. In practice the wisdom of emptiness and a serene compassion work hand in hand. But the philosophical reasons why this should be so are far from apparent. The unity between wisdom and compassion is expressed as follows in the *Vimalakīrti Sūtra:*

> A bodhisattva should regard all living beings as a wise man regards the reflection of the moon in water or as magicians regard men created by magic. He should regard them as being like a face in a mirror; like the water in a mirage . . . like the perception of color in one blind from birth . . . like the pregnancy of a barren women. . . . Precisely thus, Mañjūśrī, does a bodhisattva who realizes ultimate selflessness consider all beings.
>
> Mañjūśrī then asked further, "Noble sir, if a bodhisattva considers all living beings in such a way, how does he generate the great love toward them?"
>
> Vimalakīrti replied: "Mañjūśrī, when a bodhisattva considers all living beings in this way, he thinks: 'Just as I have realized the Dharma, so should I teach it to living beings.' Thereby, he generates the love that is truly a refuge for all living beings; the love that is peaceful because free of grasping . . . the love that is great compassion because it infuses the Mahāyāna with radiance; the love that is never exhausted because it acknowledges voidness and selflessness."[16]

The troubling feature of this vision is that it seems to leave no place for a rapport between human beings, since in their transitory human existence they are empty of any self-nature (*svabhāva*). One is asked to help and save others in the awareness that really there is no one who helps or saves, nor is there anyone who is helped and saved, and this detachment from the illusion of substantiality is supposed to make one all the more energetic and free in the work of compassion. Is there not a logical contradiction here? Does Mahāyāna, as Edward Conze thinks, take such contradictions in its stride? If there is a contradiction, it is scarcely felt in practice. The believer assumes as highest duty a sympathetic compassion with the sentient beings in their impermanency. As he knows that metaphysical doctrines are not sufficient, the inadequacy of these doctrines affects his concrete religious situation less than Western critics may imagine.

The Bodhisattva Ideal

The monks inclined to the new tendencies which led to the Mahāyāna form of Buddhism shared communal life with their confrères, and took over the early Buddhist teaching on mettā and karunā. Their most important innovation, the main characteristic doctrine of Mahāyāna, is the proclamation of the bodhisattva path. The bodhisattva, as the name indicates, is a being of enlightenment or wisdom. In its first appearances in Buddhist literature, the word designates the previous lives of the Buddha Śākyamuni, already intent on acquiring highest enlightenment and often sacrificing his life for the welfare of sentient beings. On this basis the ideal of the bodhisattva was developed. Worthy and capable of the enjoyment of fulfillment in nirvāṇa, the bodhisattva, inspired by compassion, exhausts himself in helping the sentient beings, who wander in the world of becoming, to reach the liberating enlightenment. Originally residing in supra-sensible space, he descends in self-abasement to the suffering ones. His great wisdom (*mahā-prajñā*) enables him and his great pitying compassion (*mahā-karunā*) drives him to show those fainting in darkness the way to the light.

Mahāyāna brings this ideal figure down to earth and presents it as the guiding model for the striving of disciples on the Buddha path. Emulating the bodhisattva, they cultivate wisdom and compassion. Thus the Buddhist understanding of human existence acquires the deep stamp of the bodhisattva ideal. In giving the precedence to this ideally compassionate figure over that of the arhat, Mahāyāna associates being "useful for oneself" (Sanskrit: *ātma-hitam;* Japanese: *jiri*) with being "useful for others" (Sanskrit: *para-hitam;* Japanese: *rita*), but nonetheless the attainment of wisdom retains its primacy over the cultivation of compassion, for enlightenment is regarded as the source of true compassion.

The two prominent bodhisattvas who flank the Buddha are Mañjūśrī, the bodhisattva of wisdom, and Samantabhadra, the bodhisattva of practice. But the most beloved, especially in Japan, are Kannon (Avalokiteśvara, Regarder of the Cries of the World),[17] the one who sees with loving compassion the sufferings of living beings in the world of becoming, and Jizō (Kṣitigarbha, Earth-store), originally an Indian earth divinity, but now a bodhisattva who has vowed to help sentient beings, and who grants long life, easy childbirth, fertile land, and is the protector of children. Images of Jizō, dressed as a monk, are sometimes met with at the roadside as a guide to travelers, sometimes placed in miniature as a memorial to a dead child. It is said that Śākyamuni entrusted him with the task of saving people until the enlightenment of the future Buddha Maitreya (now a bodhisattva throned in his Tuṣita Heaven) takes place in 5,670,000,000 years' time. If one thinks of Jizō, recites his name, and makes statues of him, he will come at the time of one's death and lead one to the Pure Land of Maitreya. He is represented as descending to hell to free sinners there, going beyond even Amida Buddha in unconditional mercy; hence his great popularity.[18]

Kannon is celebrated in the twenty-fifth chapter of the *Lotus Sūtra* (Sanskrit: *Saddharma-puṇḍarīka-sūtra*), a chapter which is popularly known as the *Kannon Sutra*. She (for the male figure has been feminized in China) takes the forms of thirty-three categories of beings, from Brahmans to young maidens, from gods to dragons, to save each of them. In Japan, pilgrimages to thirty-three temples corresponding to these metamorphoses of Kannon have been set up since the Edo period (1600–1868). This versatility in metamorphosis shows Kannon's mastery of skillful means (*upāya*), a notion of great importance in Mahāyāna.[19] Buddhas and bodhisattvas excel in the deployment of skillful means in order to lead the weak and ignorant to salvation.

Mahāyāna ethics, often called simply the bodhisattva ethic, center on the six (or ten) perfections (pāramitā). It is the spirit of wisdom that stamps each of the perfections or virtues with its true worth. What makes almsgiving, for example, a worthy deed? It is the spirit of wisdom in which it is performed. But equally essential is the compassionate selflessness expressed in the so-called bodhisattva vows through which the believer binds himself to earnest effort, at a solemn ceremony on the occasion of his entry on the spiritual path: "However numerous are the sentient beings that exist, I vow to save them all."

The wording of these vows sounds rather strong, if not exaggerated. Like many such high-sounding professions, they seem to take us into a land of wishful thinking and heroic resolves which has no relation to reality. To allay such misgivings, let us recall that the image of the bodhisattva derives in large part from the Jātaka legends of the Buddha's previous lives, and that these ancient Indian stories indulge an extravagance of fantasy which is astonishing to Westerners. Many Japanese Buddhists also find such fantasy alien, and have been engaged for the last thirty or forty years on demythologization of the legendary contents of their religion. Our judgment on the bodhisattva image in the Jātaka stories must begin from the horizon of ancient Indian culture. Then it becomes clear that the stories wish to convey a lesson in a style foreign to our tastes. Educated Buddhists find in the symbolic language of their traditions a teaching about the omnipotence of benevolence, the beauty of forgiveness, and the supreme value of compassion. They know that none of the bodhisattvas are historical beings, and they interpret them as embodying aspects of the Buddha. This demythologization is facilitated by the notion of skillful means.

Buddha as Father

Śākyamuni, the Buddha who has awakened to enlightenment, is often called a teacher and a physician in early accounts of his life. Only later does the designation "father" appear, exclusively in the *Lotus Sūtra,* in which the historical Buddha manifests himself as a Buddha transcending and penetrating all times and places. In the third and fourth chapters of the sūtra the Buddha compares himself to a father and speaks of his paternal care for all sentient beings. It is not surprising that this sūtra, in which believers find themselves addressed as the Buddha's children, should have attracted more veneration than any other Buddhist scripture, and become an object of trust and devotion to countless people.

Like a father moved by the deepest pity, the Buddha draws on all the resources of his wisdom to find clever means of saving the errant sentient beings. Two vivid parables show the unlimited miraculous power of the Buddha in the application of skillful means. They reveal that the driving force of all his activity is his inexhaustible compassion. The third chapter contains the parable of the burning house. In a great house, on the verge of collapsing, a fire suddenly breaks out; the flames beat high on all four sides. The master of the house stands outside in front of the door. He is told: your children are in the house and are playing contentedly. In vain the father calls out words of warning to them. Lost in their play, they do not hear him. Then he plans to apply a skillful means:

> The father proclaims to them: "The things you so love to play with are rare and hard to get. If you do not get them, you are certain to regret it later. Things like these, a variety of goat-drawn carriages, deer-drawn carriages, and ox-drawn carriages, are now outside the door for you to play with. Come out of this burning house quickly, all of you! I will give all of you what you desire." The children hear what their father says. Since rare playthings are exactly what they desire, the heart of each is emboldened. Shoving one another aside in a mad race, all together in a rush they leave the burning house.[20]

The father is overjoyed. All the children are rescued. The Buddha explains to his disciples the deep meaning of the parable:

> Śāriputra, just as that great man, seeing his children safely out of the burning house and in a place of safety, and thinking that he himself has wealth incalculable, presents his children equally with great carriages, just so in the same way does the Thus Come One (Tathāgata), being the Father of all living beings, when he sees

> incalculable thousands of millions of beings going through the gateway of the Buddha's doctrine off the painful, fearful, and precipitous pathway of the three worlds, there to gain the joy of nirvāna—just so, I say, does the Thus Come One at that time have the thought: "I have a treasure house of incalculable, limitless knowledge, strengths, various sorts of fearlessness, other such Buddhadharmas. These living beings are all my children." Then he gives the Great Vehicle equally to all, not allowing any of them to gain passage to extinction (nirvāna) for himself alone, but conveying them all to the extinction of the Thus Come One.[21]

The Great Vehicle, Mahāyāna, is the One Vehicle (Sanskrit: *ekayāna*) which replaces the three vehicles and carries all—hearers (Sanskrit: śrāvaka), self-awakenened ones (Sanskrit: *pratyekabuddha),* and bodhisattvas—to enlightenment. The Buddha gives a solemn assurance:

> I tell you, Śāriputra,
> You men
> Are all my children,
> And I am your Father.
> For kalpa upon kalpa, you
> Have been scorched by multitudinous woes,
> And I have saved you all.[22]

The fourth chapter of the *Lotus Sūtra,* the parable of an errant son whose father leads him back to his house, known as the parable of the prodigal son because of its proximity to the Lukan story (Luke 15.11–32), is based on narrative material which occurs in various forms in the Middle East. There is an extensive literature comparing the two texts, which however are too far apart in time and in place of origin to allow us, according to the present state of research, to find a dependence of one text on the other. Basic divergences in the core motifs reinforce this finding.

Here, as in the parable of the burning house, the sūtra vividly represents the application of skillful means as well as the father's compassionate care. The son who has run away from his father drifts for long years through many countries until his way takes him to the city in which his father, who has in the meantime become wealthy, resides. The father has often thought with regret of the son to whom he wants to bequeath his riches. The poor son comes seeking employment to the father's palace, but is daunted by the magnificence of the place and hastily leaves. The father has caught sight of him and sends messengers after him, who bring him back by force. Terrified, the son faints and falls to the ground. Now the father resorts to skillful means. He releases the son and allows him to undertake work removing dirt. Then comes the most moving passage of the parable:

> The father, seeing his son, was struck by both pity and amazement. Then, on another day, through a window he saw the figure of his son, weak and emaciated, wasted away, grimy and soiled with dung, dirt, and dust. Straightway he removed his necklaces, his fine outer garments, and his ornaments, and put on instead a rough, torn, dirty, tar-stained garment and, smearing dust over his body, took in his right hand a dung-shovel. Now frightful in appearance, he addressed his workmen: "You men, work! You may not slacken![23]

Having approached his son by this device, he encourages him and praises him as better than the other workers: "I have never seen you guilty of these evils, as are the other workmen. From now on you shall be like my own son."

However, the son must continue to work hard for another twenty years, until the father, knowing that he will shortly die, instructs the son on the extent of his riches, and finally in the presence of his assembled relatives and other dignitaries declares:

> Know that this is my son, begotten by me. Having forsaken me in such-and-such a city and run off, he suffered loneliness and hardship for more than fifty years. . . . He is really my son. I am really his father. Now all the treasure I have belongs to my son.[24]

In the concluding explanation the immeasurable riches of the father are interpreted as those of the Great Vehicle. The compassion of the Buddha is compared with that of the father. The Buddha-father is anxious above all to share his wealth with his son.

The *Lotus Sūtra,* a rich source of Mahāyāna Buddhology, allows the figure of the Buddha to radiate in the completeness of his perfections. The two parables cited shed light on one side of the Buddha which is extremely attractive though usually little noticed. The enlightened one takes pity on his children, the sentient beings. This legitimate extension of the characteristics of the Śākyamuni of legend was taken up in the Mahāyāna schools and lived out in religious practice. I shall now give some examples of this from Japanese Buddhism.

Compassion in Japanese Buddhism

The teaching and praxis of Japanese Buddhism is pervaded through and through with the spirit of compassionate sympathy. This is evident, for instance, in the Shingon school, one of the strongest as well as oldest currents in Japanese Buddhism. While the Mahāyāna schools claimed to have the perfect form of the Buddha's teaching, and saw earlier forms of Buddhism as provisional teachings for those who were weak of understanding, esoteric Buddhism, known as the Vajrayāna or Diamond Vehicle, in turn considered itself superior to the other Mahāyāna schools. According to Kūkai (posthumously known as Kōbō Daishi, 774–835), the founder of the Shingon sect, the "true word" (*shingon*) is preached not by the Buddha in his manifestation body (*nirmāṇakāya*) as the historical Śākyamuni, but by the dharmakāya Buddha himself, as he expounds for his own enjoyment his innermost spiritual experience.[25] Kūkai is inspired by a key statement at the beginning of the *Mahāvairocana Sūtra,* a basic text of Buddhist Tantrism, composed in India and generally assigned to the middle of the seventh century:

> "The enlightened mind is the cause, great compassion is the root, and [the use of] skillful means is the ultimate." In other words,

> enlightenment is attainable because of the originally enlightened mind; the basic character of the Buddha Wisdom is its capacity for compassionate acts; and the perfection of the wisdom can be judged by whether or not it works freely to help others grow spiritually.[26]

The disciple vows "not to go without benefiting all sentient beings." Kūkai comments:

> To violate this is to go against the spirit of the Four Embracing Acts [charity, kind speech, beneficial acts, and adapting oneself to others]. A bodhisattva should practice the Four Embracing Acts and universally embrace all sentient beings, providing them with the conditions which will interest them in the Way.[27]

In the schools inspired by the *Lotus Sūtra,* as in the sūtra itself, wisdom and compassion are the defining traits of an exalted, majestic conception of the Buddha. In the Kamakura period (1185–1333), a time of Buddhist renewal, Nichiren preached the *Lotus Sūtra* as the only salvation in the Latter Days of the Law (mappō). His apocalyptic message of warning grew milder in his later years, becoming one of helpful and generous guidance, as we can see from the letters he wrote in old age from the solitude of his retreat on Mount Minobu. The compassionate spirit of the message of Nichiren, a man close to the people, can be found today among the numerous followers of the modern popular religions that have emerged from the Nichiren school. A leading figure in one such movement, the Sōka Gakkai, once explained to me during a tour of the grounds of Taisekiji temple that even the method of *shakubuku*—a controversial form of intensive proselytism, then under heavy attack from Japanese society at large—was based on Great Compassion (mahā-karunā). Compassion urges us to shatter error, even by violence.

The other schools of the Kamakura period had their own style of practicing the bodhisattva ethic of compassion. In Zen the masters of the golden age of T'ang-dynasty China had combined severity often bordering on ferocity with well-wishing compassion.[28] In the kōan collection *Wu-wen kuan* (The Gateless Barrier), popular in Japan as the *Mumonkan* and used in many Zen halls, there is the story of Tung-shan menaced with being beaten three-score times with a stick. Hakuin (1685–1768), who renewed Japanese Zen during the Edo period, received equally rough treatment: "The master twisted my nose with his fingers. . . . 'You poor hole-dwelling devil!' he cried."[29]

This tradition lives on into the present. The guidance given by an enlightened master (Japanese: *rōshi*), who combines severity with warm benevolence, is seen as a work of compassion. The disciple may be rejected at first, may be rudely handled, and only accepted after persistent pleading, he may be given kōans, scolded, struck, or he may after long experience be encouraged and put on the way to further attainments—in all cases the master's actions are motivated by compassion for the disciple's suffering. Contemporary Zen disciples often attest to the compassion of their masters by their words of sincere gratitude.

The Pure Land Buddhism of Hōnen and Shinran is based on taking refuge in the forty-eight vows of Amida Buddha, listed in the *Larger Pure Land Sūtra*. These vows spring from the immeasurable compassion of Amida, and they assure final rescue to the sentient beings afflicted by sufferings and entangled in errors. From the life and light which constitute his being, as his two names Amitāyus and Amitābha indicate, unlimited compassion flows down to the samsaric world. The images of Amida's coming to the world, the deeply religious works of art known as Amida raigō paintings, have aroused and strengthened the trusting faith of countless East Asians. These believers, linked to their Buddha by the invocation of his name, the nembutsu, and gazing on his form, make the imitation of his compassion the leading motive of their behavior, sometimes to the extent of almost forgetting the other aspects of morality. Though Shinran gave up the monastic obligation of celibacy, he urged his followers to practice the five Buddhist precepts as a testimony of gratitude for Amida's grace; thus even in this, its mildest form, the Buddhist tradition in Japan never degenerated into amoralism.

Against the individualism of earlier Pure Land thought, Shinran brought out the solidarity of all beings in the attainment of salvation; however, the bodhisattva's concern for the salvation of all is a feature of existence in the Pure Land, not in this present life in which one is bound by sin and totally incapable of helping others.[30] Unconcerned with this doctrinal difficulty, many Pure Land Buddhists practice a bodhisattva-like compassion for their fellow sinners. Here is one of D.T. Suzuki's tales of the myōkōnin:

> When a man heard noise going on in his yard, he looked out and saw the boys of the neighborhood climbing up one of the trees in his orchard, trying to steal the fruit. The man quietly went out and put a ladder underneath the boys who were up in the tree, then he quietly returned to his house. . . . This devotee, this myōkōnin, fears that when the children try to come down stealthily out of the tree, so the master won't know they are stealing his fruit, they might slip, fall down to the ground, and get hurt. His impulse is to prevent them from being harmed, not to save his property.[31]

These indications of the central place of compassion in Japanese Buddhism have a special actuality in our days. At a time when a new awareness of the unity of humankind on this small planet brings near to all of us the nameless sufferings of millions of our fellow-humans, every religion is seeking in its origins and traditions inspiration for cooperation in solidarity in the service of suffering humanity. In Japan, Buddhism is called to raise anew the banner of compassionate sympathy.

The Dialogue with Christian Love

Comparisons between Buddhist benevolence or compassion and Christian love have, like the general encounter of the two religions, passed through various phases. At first the apologetic attitude prevailed, with the Christians paying careful attention to the irreducible differences between the two ideals. Today the stress is more on what they have in common. Both approaches are valid and can conduce to mutual understanding.

Christian love is a theological virtue, which is sustained by a reference to God in faith, and which gives practical expression to this faith. The New Testament reduces the moral law to a single commandment, which has two aspects: love of God and love of neighbor. This love is personal: love of God is a response to the personal love of a personal God, love of neighbor is born in a personal encounter with the brother or sister created in the image of God. By and large, the personhood of God and the status of the human person have been taken as unproblematic givens in Christian tradition. Buddhism alerts us to difficulties and dangers in our way of thinking of personhood, but conversely the Christian witness to the value of personhood and to the ultimately personal nature of the absolute reality can help overcome shortcomings in Buddhist thinking.

The Buddhist-Christian dialogue prefers, however, to focus on the existential and practical level. It is here that the most promising points of contact for interreligious dialogue are to be found. This is only to be expected, given that benevolence towards one's fellow humans is at the heart of both religions, however differently articulated in the differing doctrinal presuppositions. The dialogue can best begin with the two specific themes that have most brought Buddhists and Christians closer in our time: non-violence and tolerance.

Non-violence (*ahiṃsā*) comes with the Indian roots of Buddhism. We noted above the strong connection of compassion with the first Buddhist commandment, not to kill. In ancient Indian morality this commandment is motivated chiefly by the inviolability of life. The Buddha bases it on a variant of the Golden Rule: "My thought has wandered through the world in all directions; yet I have not met with anything that was dearer to anyone than himself; therefore let him, who desires his own advantage, not harm another."[32] From the start the Buddhists stressed the practical relevance of non-violence for the happiness and peace of humankind. The pragmatic import of the teaching is clear from the *Dhammapada:*

> "He reviled me! He struck me!
> He defeated me! He robbed me!"
> They who gird themselves up with this,
> For them enmity is not quelled.
> Not by enmity are enmities quelled,
> Whatever the occasion here.
> By the absence of enmity are they quelled.
> With absence of wrath one would conquer the wrathful one;
> With good, one would conquer the bad one;
> With giving one would conquer the stingy one;
> With truth, the one speaking falsehood.[33]

The Buddha's concern is to root out enmities in an effective way, creating peace and happiness on earth, and thus, in a pragmatic spirit, leading people to what really profits them. This attitude shaped the actions of the historical Buddha and also those of King Aśoka (third century BCE) who, after the conquest of the kingdom of Kaliṅga, was so shaken by the sufferings of the conquered that he vowed never to take up arms again and kept his vow to the end—an exception among the mighty of the earth.

Buddhist compassion also gives rise to tolerance. The Buddha is portrayed as the most tolerant of teachers, keeping his distance from doctrinal disputes, and warning the disciples to keep their self-control when provoked by the calumnies of outsiders. Both Buddhists and Christians have learned much about tolerance from the thinkers of the Enlightenment, but this lesson finds an echo in the depths of their own traditions. Tolerance implies no surrender or devaluation of truth; rather, it is the confidence of standing fast in the truth that frees one to be tolerant towards those who do not share it, in the awareness that one's human way of possessing the truth is necessarily limited and imperfect, and that it is the birthright of all human beings to seek the truth in freedom. The unity of the planet today has made pluralism an established part of our lives, demanding of us an unprecedented ability to respect different religions and world-views.

In conclusion: for Buddhists compassion is not just one virtue among others, but the very peak of the Buddhist way of life, and one of the foundations of the religion from the very start. This defining ideal of Buddhism is embodied in the Buddha, the bodhisattvas, and the Buddhist saints. The philosophical systems developed in early Buddhism and in Mahāyāna Buddhism were unable to provide a satisfactory philosophical illumination of this topic. Christian love, which has also found convincing embodiment in countless lives, cannot be explained in philosophical terms either, though its foundations in divine transcendence are clear.

V

Buddhist Meditation

We have seen that the themes of suffering (dukkha), non-self, knowledge, faith, and compassion resonate with Christian preoccupations. But it is in the practice of meditation that Buddhist religion reaches its supreme expression, and it is here, too, that the Buddhist-Christian dialogue has found its most substantial basis.

Buddhists are never so actively cooperative, so exemplary and so generous, as when they share their wisdom about meditation and initiate people into its practice. No other aspect of Buddhism has aroused the same interest and eager desire to learn on the part of Westerners, however much this desire may sometimes be mixed up with a superficial search for exotica or esoterica. This chapter in Buddhist-Christian exchange has been chiefly a matter of practice. But a more reflective and theoretical grasp of the place of meditation in Buddhism is not a useless addition to this; indeed it is indispensible for its lucid and fruitful continuation. Such reflection can also allay some of the philosophical and theological misgivings that Westerners often have about Buddhist meditation.

MINDFULNESS

In all branches of Buddhism, meditation is a core practice, though in a variety of methods. One may assess some of these methods as of lesser value than others, but it would be a mistake to think that from the value of the method one can measure the genuineness of the experience attained with its assistance. An earnest practitioner using a less effective method can reach greater depths than one who has a better method but less zeal.

It is an exaggeration to call Buddhism a kind of Yoga, for this description misses essential features of the Buddhist path of salvation. But it is true that the meditational exercises of early Buddhism, which live on in Theravāda Buddhism today, took over and integrated many important elements from Yoga: body postures, breathing, control of the senses, stilling of the activities of the mind and imagination. The body is as central to Buddhist meditation as to Yoga. Indeed meditation without the body is unknown to the Eastern religions. But Theravāda does not insist on a particular posture. In each of the four postures, walking, standing, sitting, and lying, one can cultivate mindfulness (Pali: *sati*), which is the attitude that is most central to Theravāda meditation.

The only meditation text in the Pali Canon, the *Satipaṭṭhāna-sutta,* is still the basic document for Theravāda meditation today. As a canonical writing, presented as a speech of the Buddha himself, this "Discourse on the Foundations of Mindfulness" enjoys the highest authority. Its status is enhanced by the Buddha's insistence, in the introductory words, that it indicates the only way to the purification of beings, the overcoming of suffering, and the realization of nirvāṇa. The outstanding position of this sūtra in Buddhist history is attested by its wide distribution and the fond esteem in which the faithful have held it. In the West, too, it is prized by the meditation movement, and is easily accessible in the translation and commentary of Nyanaponika Thera, a German who became a Buddhist monk in Sri Lanka.[1] Other classics of Theravāda meditation and doctrine are the two treatises *Vimuttimagga* by Upatissa[2] and the *Visuddhimagga* by Buddhaghosa.[3]

Sati, meaning mindfulness or awareness, denotes a serene reflection on reality, which produces salutary effects. Many references in the Pali Canon underscore its value. "Right mindfulness" (*sammāsati*) is the seventh step of the Eightfold Path and the first of the seven branches of enlightenment (*bojjhaṅga*). As an activity of recollection, mindfulness refers both to the past (calling to mind) and to the present (keeping in mind). In the present, it makes present the given realities that ever exist only momentarily, and in each instance it apprehends their coming to be and passing away. Impermanence, an intrinsic feature of all being, is concretely experienced by the meditator who keeps in view in alert observation a constantly altering flux of similar happenings.

The *Satipaṭṭhāna-sutta* names four "foundations," which constitute the whole of reality: the body, the feelings, the states of consciousness, and the mental contents. For the body, one is to observe inhaling and exhaling; the four postures of the body; the four elements (earth, water, heat, wind) in the body; and lastly the dissolution factors, in nine cemetary contemplations. "And how, monks, does a monk dwell practising body-contemplation on the body?"[4] This opening question reveals the importance given to the body in satipaṭṭhāna meditation. Practitioners are urged to dedicate themselves to the practice of bare attention to the bodily processes in which they are caught up. One must only see, only hear, only sense, with the organs of the body, putting aside reflection, disposing oneself receptively in every respect. Evaluations, if allowed, would inevitably attach themselves to this bare attending, and spoil its purity. Among the functions of the body, breathing enjoys primacy. The question quoted above is answered as follows:

> Herein, monks, a monk having gone to the forest, to the foot of a tree, or to an empty place, sits down cross-legged, keeps his body erect and his mindfulness alert. Just mindful he breathes in and mindful he breathes out. Breathing in a long breath, he knows "I breathe in a long breath"; breathing out a long breath, he knows "I breathe out a long breath"; breathing in a short breath, he knows "I breathe in a short breath"; breathing out a short breath, he knows "I breathe out a short breath."[5]

Meditative mindfulness is subsequently applied to feelings and states of consciousness which stand in direct or indirect relation to the body; they can be pleasant, unpleasant, or also neither pleasant nor unpleasant, and it is as thus classified that one takes note of them. One notes the feelings which arise, in close conjunction with bodily states, identifying them as pleasant, unpleasant, or indifferent. The states of consciousness, which either help or hinder the production of salutary effects, are also simply noted without reflection. In the language of modern psychology we would call these states of consciousness psychosomatic, as they have mental and bodily components. They have a closer relation to the path of salvation insofar as negative states of consciousness, such as ignorance, infatuation, anger and so on, block spiritual progress, whereas higher ones can foster it. Finally, among the mental contents important points of doctrine, such as the five skandhas or the Four Noble Truths, are listed. Spontaneously arising thoughts are merely noted. The meditation exercise confines itself to bare attention.

The observed processes are grasped as a whole as well as in their constituent elements. Thus, not resting satisfied with noting the four postures of the body—walking, standing, sitting, lying—one mindfully analyzes each of these postures into its parts; for instance: "I walk, that is, I lift the right foot, stretch the right foot forward, let the right foot fall, touch the ground with the right foot, stand on both feet, lift the left foot." Another example may make clear the many-layered quality of observant analysis. I see a wound on the arm and observe: The arm is a part of the body; it belongs to the first of the four foundations, namely the body. The pain of the arm is a feeling; it belongs to the second group, namely feelings. I sense the pain, that is, I notice the psychical state of pain, a state of consciousness, which belongs to the third group. There supervenes a fourth state, ego-consciousness, the "ego-illusion," which misleads the mind, and in certain circumstances creates negative karma that hinders salutary attainment.

Initially sensed as monotonously uniform, the act of simply registering, uninterrupted by any movement of emotion, creates a state of tranquillity, which is scarcely noticed by the practitioner at first. Concentrated mindfulness issues in an even state of calm. As one puts away all movements, whether cognitional or emotive, which attach themselves to this state of consciousness, there prevails the deep tranquillity of distance from all life processes. In accord with the doctrinal heritage of the Pali Canon, satipaṭṭhāna meditation stresses above all distance from the ego and the ego-conscious functions. It is the pressing task of all meditative effort to release one from ego-related representations and feelings, and this is achieved in meditation precisely by subjecting to the observing gaze whatever life processes impinge on awareness. The existential differention between the empirical ego and the ungraspable, unobjectifiable true self, which we suggested in chapter two, is experienced most clearly in this activity of attention, as the practitioner calmly notes the surface psychosomatic ego-levels, and undoes their claims to represent the true depths of the self. These depths are not to be thought of as pure spirit, but as a more integrated body-spirit unity.

The Theravāda method of mindfulness is connected with the dharma theory, according to which the world and the ego consist of factors of existence, or dharmas, which from moment to moment are coming to be and passing away. In meditation, attention to these factors of existence destroys the representation of a permanent ego, which is a habitual part of our everyday consciousness. No "I" passes before my gaze, but the passing processes consist of a multiplicity of physical and psychical factors, analysis of which reveals the transitoriness of all things, including one's empirical ego. Thus meditation makes unmistakably vivid the First Noble Truth and the doctrine of non-self.

Through sustained conscious meditation one reaches a high degree of concentration. The final goal is to attain the clear gaze (Pali: *vipassanā*) which is defined as "the flashing forth of an intuitive knowledge of the impermanence, painfulness, and impersonality of all corporal and mental phenomena of existence."[6] This is associated with another method, oriented to a state of mental tranquillity (Pali: *samatha*). The "development of mental calm" (*samatha-bhāvanā*) occurs through the "development of concentration" (*samādhi-bhāvanā*). The mind is calmed through concentrations in which the outer world entirely fades out, and even psychical activities, especially those of thought, are stilled. The Pali Canon distinguishes the clear gaze and tranquillity of mind as different fruits of meditation, but it does not separate them. An intuitive and ecstatic moment is contained in both, giving proof that a higher state of consciousness has been attained.

As one regularly practices this calm attending to the phenomena arising in one's mind, one grows in serenity and inner equilibrium. The practice of mindfulness has an influence on the whole of one's life. At certain times, mindfulness is practiced in a methodical way. But in the midst of everyday activities, too, it should never be abandoned. One must strive to be mindful in all one's activity. The disposition attained and cultivated in methodical practice can be applied to any activity whatsoever.

In regard to the effects of mindfulness, we note a remarkable correspondence between the two representative ways of meditation, satipaṭṭhāna and Zen. Satipaṭṭhāna meditation aims to know all life-processes and all things just as they are. The classical Chinese Zen masters of the T'ang dynasty led their disciples to give up all superfluous adjuncts and to see "things just as they are" (a well-known Zen phrase). This correspondence even on the level of phraseology is not fortuitous but a contact in essentials, at the level of the basic concern of Buddhist meditation with the experience of reality without any supplement.

Theravāda meditation has known some variations over the centuries, such as the "New Burmese method of meditation" developed recently. Indeed the method expounded in the Pali Canon could itself be seen, like the dharma philosophy, as a deviation from the primitive Buddhist teaching. We have every reason to believe that the Buddha and his disciples practiced meditation, but we do not know what method they followed. Theravādins see the method of attention and clear-sightedness (*sati-vipassanā*) as the one followed at the outset of

Buddhism, and they consider it to be diametically opposed to Christian prayer. The latter they know mainly in the form of prayers of petition, which they reject together with what they take to be the thoroughgoing anthropomorphism of the Christian idea of a creator God.

There is much to be said about the connection between meditation and prayer. In their point of departure and their goals the two are undoubtedly different, yet there is no need to set them in irreconcilable opposition. Certainly, the dharma theory, insofar as it denies not only the empirical ego but the true self, is in contradiction with basic insights and experiences of the Christian worldview. Yet in Christian spirituality, too, inner concentration is striven for, and concentration exercises of neutral content can have a place. The self-possession and self-control that are achieved through concentration are a desirable possession for all religions.

We may go a step farther. Among the meditative techniques transmitted in Theravāda spirituality, there is one that may be said to meet Christian prayer halfway. We described in the last chapter the practice of the four Brahma dwellings, in which the monk radiates the force of benevolence, compassion, sympathetic joy, and equanimity in the four directions, filled with the wish that all sentient beings be free from care, illness, and pain and attain the peace of nirvāṇa. An essential difference from Christian prayer is that this wish is directed to no higher being; yet it is remarkable that the one wishing is certain of the fulfillment of his wish, and does not regard it as a meaningless activity. This seems to imply a confidence that reality is ultimately gracious. Does this not suggest that one who practices such meditation is drawing near to a transcendent reality?

The final goal of meditation for Theravāda, as for the Pali Canon Buddhism on which it is based, is to reach nirvāṇa, and not only after death but already in this present life. The experience of nirvāṇa is inexpressible; the one who enjoys it has clear-sighted insight into the impermanence of all things, and intuitively grasps the Four Noble Truths. Nirvāṇa by its very nature transcends all concepts and representations.

It is described as the state of final release and is brought near to hearers of the Buddhist preaching by metaphors evocative of happiness and serenity. The effects of peace, joy, and bliss experienced in meditation are also pointers to the quality of nirvāṇa.

Meditation in Mahāyāna Buddhism

The rise of Mahāyāna did not create a break in the Buddhist tradition of meditation, for the new movement took over the early Buddhist meditative practices. Representatives of Mahāyāna for a long time lived in the same community with monks of strict traditional observance. However the Mahāyānists began to develop variant methods of meditation which corresponded better with their doctrinal vision and which were based on the Mahāyāna sutras.

Among the lesser-known Mahāyāna sutras are a number of texts devoted entirely to meditation. Many of these were translated into Chinese and shaped the religious atmosphere in which a culture of meditation crystallized in various sects of Chinese Buddhism.

The teaching of the *Yogācārabhūmi-sūtra,* a Vijñānavādin text from the early period of Chinese Buddhism, represents the transition from the Hearers' Vehicle to the Mahāyāna. This extensive sutra was translated into Chinese by Dharmaraksa (233–310); the original Sanskrit is not extant. It deals at length with meditation, mapping the stages of a meditative ascent. Equally important for the beginnings of Mahāyāna meditation is the *Dharmatara-dhyāna-sūtra* translated by Buddhabhadra around 413, which is a systematic presentation of meditation.[7] The annals of early Chinese Buddhist history also tell of the activities of masters of meditation, from India, Central Asia, and China alike.

The budding Mahāyāna meditation was first brought into systematic form on Chinese soil in the T'ien-t'ai school, especially in the work of its third patriarch, Chih-i (538–97). Chih-i, traditionally known as the "great teacher of T'ien-t'ai," is rightly regarded as the real founder of the tradition. From his master, the second patriarch, Hui-ssu (515–77), he inherited a glowing reverence for the *Lotus Sūtra* as well as a high estimation of meditation, confirmed by his own experience. Characteristic of the T'ien-t'ai system propagated in Chih-i's voluminous writings is the close bond between doctrine and meditation, teaching and practice. His three major works are records of his teaching at Ch'ang-an, the capital: *Sentences and Phrases of the Lotus Sūtra (Fa-hua wen-chü)* an extensive commentary on the text of the sutra; *The Profound Meaning of the Lotus Sutra (Fa-hua hsüan-i)* a systematic exposition of the sūtra's doctrines; and *The Great Calming and Contemplation (Mo-ho chih-kuan)* a vast treatise on meditation. The *Great Calming* is a voluminous work, not easily surveyed. It was the object of years of strenuous study by the monks on Mount T'ien-t'ai, the headquarters of the school, and later at the head temple of the Japanese version of T'ien-t'ai, called Tendai, situated on Mount Hiei northwest of Kyoto. In this century its complexities have been unraveled by Japanese scholars and more recently by Western ones as well.

The *Great Calming* has a preface by Kuan-ting (561–623), chief disciple of Chih-i and his successor as patriarch, to whom we owe the redaction of the master's writings. Here Kuan-ting names three kinds of meditation: perfect and sudden, indeterminate, and step-by-step or gradual. The contrast between sudden and gradual meditation is common in Chinese Buddhism. The indeterminacy dealt with by introducing the middle stage reflects the variety among practitioners, who choose elements from the sudden and gradual approaches in accord with their temperament, gifts, and inclination. This indeterminate meditation is the subject of a one-volume work, and another early work deals with gradual meditation, treating early Buddhist meditation methods from the Mahāyāna standpoint. In the following we confine ourselves to the basic text of Tendai meditation, the *Great Calming,* which presents the perfect, sudden meditation in every detail of preparation, practice, and fruition, along with elements of gradual meditation.

The purpose of the perfect, sudden meditation is to realize the fundamental Mahāyāna insight into the identity of nirvāṇa and saṃsāra, the cosmic Buddha body and the phenomenal world. The *Great Calming* crystallizes this vision in the formula of "the trichiliocosm in a moment of consciousness" (Chinese: *i-nien san-ch'ien*). The trichiloscosm (three thousand worlds) is the world of common experience, which, when properly viewed, is identical with the absolute, with emptiness. "This Truth was not to be attained by mere intellectual comprehension, but rather through a direct religious experience, a process quite beyond verbalization, in which the practitioner became at one with the Truth itself."[8]

The Mādhyamika tradition had distinguished ultimate from provisional reality or truth, ascribing to the latter realm whatever can be put into words and concepts. Put simply, the ultimate truth is that all phenomena are radically empty of any stable substantiality, a truth that is finally ineffable, and that can be grasped only by moving beyond the conceptual realm. The provisional truth, in contrast, is that which makes sense amid the conventions of worldly existence, and it includes all the formulations and conceptualizations of Buddhist doctrine itself. For Chih-i the provisional signifies a "non-denial of the empirical world,"[9] despite the inaccessibility of ultimate reality to our everyday empirical and logical categories. Chih-i adds a third level, in his doctrine of the threefold truth—the empty, the provisional, and the middle—a central structural principle of T'ien-t'ai thought; the threefold contemplation (Chinese: *san-kuan*) is the subjective aspect of this triad.

The "middle" refers to the ability to hold absolute and provisional together and to realize their identity.

> The recognition of the perfectly balanced codependence of the void (kū) and the provisional (*ke*) was Tendai's third stage, that of the middle (*chū*). The middle is not a position midway between the other two but the holding of both in a state of dynamic and equalized tension. Each way of looking at things is valid but only because the other is also true; each side gives existence and function to the other.[10]

In attaining the middle, the mind is one with ultimate reality, since mind and reality cannot be distinguished. "The cognizing mind and the cognized objects are interdependent, and the sphere in which they exist in a state of interdependence is a third realm transcending both of them. The attainment of Truth or Buddhahood (the two are identical), consists of a transfer of self to this third realm, not of an intellectual standing-off-and-looking-at-it."[11]

Another influential, though rather abstract, formula of Chih-i's is the "six identities," which points up the parallelism between doctrine and practice, and identifies the immanence of the Buddha nature in all sentient beings as the point of departure and the point of arrival of meditation. The path of meditation begins with a merely intellectual knowledge of one's Buddhahood. Then as one's behavior and mental state are gradually brought into correspondence with this truth, wisdom becomes increasingly prominent until one attains the final fruit, at the sixth stage, realizing one's Buddhahood and the ultimate nature of reality as Buddha nature.[12] Famed for his modesty, Chih-i never claimed to have attained this highest identity, although his career was distinguished by at least two powerful experiences of enlightenment. The grading of meditative stages inculcates both confidence and modesty: "The existence of identity erases self-depreciation and doubt while the existence of six gradations erases arrogance."[13]

In his early writings Chih-i calls all kinds of meditation ch'an—that is, dhyāna or zen—but in the mature late work, the *Great Calming,* he introduces the term *chih-kuan* (Japanese: *shikan),* which became normative in T'ien-t'ai. The two Chinese characters correspond to the Sanksrit words samatha and vipaśyanā, meaning "quietude, tranquillity, absence of passions" and "clear knowledge, insight, inward vision" respectively. Even imperfect stages of meditation are called chih-kuan, but in its full sense the expression denotes the vision, attained in enlightenment, of the identity of all reality with the Buddha.

In the vast repertory of the *Great Calming* two paths to ultimate enlightenment stand out. In the early books there is a schema of four practices, which are preliminary to the "perfect and sudden" meditation.

> There are many methods of practice, but we may summarize them under four sorts: (1) constantly sitting, (2) constantly walking, (3)

> part walking, part sitting, and (4) neither walking nor sitting. By referring to them collectively as "samādhis," we mean that one thereby attunes, rectifies, and stabilizes the mind. The *Ta-chih-tu-lun* (Great Perfection of Wisdom Treatise) says, "Skillfully to fix the mind on one spot and abide there without shifting—that is called samādhi." The Dharmadhātu is a "single spot," and through true discernment you can abide there and never stray from it.[14]

In the Indian context the word "samādhi" refers to an advanced meditative experience, but Chih-i uses it for meditative practice in the wide sense. These four practices constitute (along with some brief manuals of Chih-i and his master, which they summarize) the earliest guidelines for meditation in Mahāyāna. As concrete directives, their influence extended beyond T'ien-t'ai to the other Chinese Mahāyāna schools. The first three practices associate a bodily posture with mental concentration on unity with the Buddha. The first recommends the classical lotus position (Sanskrit: *padmāsana;*), control of breathing, and concentration through the stilling of thoughts and images. Objects of cognition are not completely banished, but the practitioner is to identify them with the ultimate reality of the dharma realm (*dharmadhātu*).

The description of the first exercise (also known as "one-practice samādhi") links its precise instructions to the metaphysical goal of the exercise:

> Sit constantly, without walking, standing, or lying down. . . . For a period of ninety days sit in the proper position, legs crossed, the neck and backbone perfectly straight, neither moving nor wavering, not drooping nor leaning on anything. . . . Just sit and rectify your thoughts. Dispel evil thoughts and discard disordered fantasies. Mix in no mental activity and do not grasp mentally at forms. Just identify the objects of cognition with the dharmadhātu and rest your thought in the dharmadhātu alone. . . . If you are confident that there is nothing that is not the Buddha's teaching, then there is no earlier and no later, no knower or expounder of the teaching. . . . Neither existent nor inexistent, neither knower

> nor nonknower, dwell then where no dwelling is possible, . . . in the perfectly quiescent dharmadhātu where all the Buddhas dwell.[15]

There are two approaches to this practice: one may either directly contemplate the dharmadhātu, or the dharma body of the Buddha, or one may concentrate on the name, image, or merits of a particular Buddha if the first approach is too exhausting. "The radical approach of complete 'non-abiding' and immediate identification with the Dharmadhātu and the expedient approach of fixing the mind on the Buddha's form and reciting his name were intended to function in close support of one another."[16]

The "constantly walking samādhi" (also known as "the samādhi wherein one finds oneself standing face to face with all the Buddhas of the present age"), as an alternative to the first one, shows that no particular posture is unconditionally required for meditation. In this exercise, the practitioner, after ritual washing and changing clothes, circumambulates an altar dedicated to Amitābha Buddha during ninety days, never leaving the meditation hall. In Indian Buddhism the circumambulation of a temple or, especially, a stūpa is a favorite practice. As he walks, the practitioner is to keep his attention fixed on Amitābha, visualizing the thirty-two bodily marks which manifest his glory. Eventually, the visualizing yields to a more interior contemplation, in which one realizes that "this Buddha is simply mind perceiving mind."[17] Whereas the first samādhi points forward to Zen by its insistence on sitting erect, the devotional element here links up with the Pure Land *Meditation Sūtra,* a text known to Chih-i. This sūtra had inspired the ardent Amida veneration of the White Lotus Society of Mount Lu, founded by the Chinese monk and nobleman Hui-yüan (344–416). Its members sought to attain visions of the Buddha of the Pure Land through intense meditation. But Chih-i uses such visualization only as a step to the insight into emptiness, which T'ien-t'ai took over from the *Perfection of Wisdom* sūtras.

The "part walking, part sitting" exercise unites the bodily postures of the first two practices. Normally, the practitioner first walks about the meditation hall one hundred and twenty times, then sits in the lotus posture, and after an interval again resumes his walking. (Chih-i gives no special role to the postures of standing and lying down.) This samādhi has two forms. In the first, ritual objects are identified with doctrinal notions, while one recites *dhāranī* (magic formulas) from a Tantric sūtra. The ceremonies of purification associated with this practice are particularly elaborate. Before entering into samādhi the practitioner requires the appearence in a dream of one of the twelve dream kings, for which he makes a persistent petition. The practice is begun under the guidance of an experienced master, and it includes ritual prostrations and repentance (reflection on and confession of faults) as well as the dhāranī recitation. It lasts seven days, but can be extended to a much longer period. During the recitation of dhāranī and mantra, or "sacred words," the practitioner's attention is directed to emptiness and the Middle Way: a combination that is typical of Tantric-influenced T'ien-t'ai meditation. However, if the practitioner finds this too strenuous, he can focus on phenomenal features of the activity at hand.

The second form of this samādhi is based on the *Lotus Sūtra.* Again, preliminary rituals are required, including five purifications. While walking, the practitioner recites the *Lotus Sūtra,* and he sits in deep silence. The exercise lasts three weeks and leads, when successful, to a vision of the bodhisattva Samantabhadra as described in the last chapter of the *Lotus Sūtra.* An alternative form of this focuses on the emptiness of all phenomena.

The "neither walking nor sitting samādhi" is on a higher plane than the other three and receives the most attention. It is known as the "samādhi of awakening to the nature of thought" or "samādhi of following one's own thought," expressions derived from the *Perfection of Wisdom* and *Lotus* sūtras. This meditation is bound to no body posture. It reaches out to all objects and situations of everyday life, to embrace them comprehensively and to bring to perfection the activity of "viewing the mind" which is the aim of all four kinds of meditation. "Your own mind contains the whole of the Buddha's teachings," declares Chih-i. "It is via the mind that Buddhas attain liberation." "When mind sees itself, it is the Buddha; mind is the Buddha mind, it is my own self."[18] Unlike the other practices, this one does not promote ritual or devotional activities, and can lead to a presumptuous disregard for such activities, and even for the moral precepts. Chih-i warns that it is not for everyone and insists on the importance of morality (śīla) and the practice of the six perfections. Of the four samādhis, the first and second were commonly practiced in T'ien-t'ai tradition, and they were also taught at meditation halls on Mount Hiei.

The other meditative path given prominence in main part of the *Great Calming* concerns the ten modes of discernment and ten spheres of discernment (or object-fields), and brings us directly into the realm of "perfect and sudden" meditation. One begins with the highest of the ten modes of contemplation, "viewing the object as inconceivable" (*acintya*), applying it to the sphere of phenomenal reality. If one needs or wishes to practice the other ninety-nine possible combinations of mode with sphere, these are all sustained by and completed in the "perfect and sudden" contemplation of the everyday world as the ungraspable absolute. As Kuan-ting states: "There is nothing that is not the ultimate reality."[19] In Chih-i's outlook, based on the *Perfection of Wisdom* sūtras, the ultimate reality cannot properly be an object of meditation, since it has no marks or features at all. It is attained by the overcoming of all dualisms and objectifications.

Chih-i was aware of the unsurpassed stature of his system, which he describes as "rounded" or perfect. It embraces Tantrism, Zen, vinaya and Pure Land—the four principal elements of Mahāyāna Buddhism—not only in its doctrinal scaffolding but in meditative practice. The influence of T'ien-t'ai on the subsequent history of Buddhist meditation can hardly be overstated. "Ch'an was forced to grow in the shadow of Chih-i's stupendous systematization of Mahāyāna methods of meditation and cannot be fully understood without reference to his work."[20] The T'ien-t'ai synthesis was further elaborated by Saichō (767–822) on

Mount Hiei in Japan, providing a fertile doctrinal platform for Japanese Buddhism until the renewal movements of the Kamakura period brought out individual strands in sharper profile.

TANTRISM: SHINGON

The two contrasting styles of meditation brought together in T'ien-t'ai—the image-based mandala meditation and the word-based nembutsu meditation—have their homes in Buddhist Tantrism and the Pure Land school respectively.[21] The mandala meditation is oriented to the cosmos. A mandala, literally "circle," is a round shape consisting of one or more concentric circles which contain smaller circles, triangles, or rectangles. Each part of the design is a well-rounded unity and the whole represents the universe. The mandala plays a central role in Buddhist Tantrism, which flourished first in North India and Tibet, then spread across China and Korea as far as Japan, where it subsists today in the Shingon school. In Shingon as in Tibetan lamaism the mandala, representing the cosmos as the holy, pure Buddha-body, is the center of cult and meditation.

This school reveres as the highest Buddha Mahāvairocana, "the great enlightener," called "the perfected one of the great sun," or Dainichi Nyorai in Japan, where he has been identified with the indigenous sun-goddess Amaterasu, the highest divinity of the Shinto pantheon. He is seen as primal ground and lord of the cosmos, containing all reality in himself. He transcends all duality and integrates the polarity of beings into a unitary whole. His might is manifested in the two mandalas of the matrix world (Sanskrit: *garbhadhātu;* Japanese: *taizōkai*) and the diamond world (Sanskrit: *vajradhātu;* Japanese: *kongōkai*), which symbolize the masculine and feminine poles. Kūkai, the founder of Shingon, received these mandalas from his Chinese teacher Hui-kuo (746–74), a disciple of the famed patriarch Amoghavajra (705–74), and brought them to Japan as the precious heritage of his residence in China. The two mandalas are the center of religious practice in Shingon. The mandalas represent Buddhas, bodhisattvas, and supernatural beings in a grid layout. Mandalas are more than objects of meditation or aids to meditation. They symbolize the goal, the Buddha, summoning the initiate to advance in meditation to the state of complete unity with the Buddha. Carrying an aura of sacredness, they bring their message home to the senses.

Recently the psychological effectiveness of mandala meditation has attracted the attention of Western scholars. Christians are rediscovering their own tradition of "image meditation," cultivated from ancient times. Most famous is the cosmic meditation image of the Swiss saint, Nicholas of Flüe (1417–87), which has inspired an important movement of meditation.

Seeking to awake to his true self, the Buddhist meditator explores the ideal cosmos that the mandala represents in microcosmic form. The German Lama Anagarika Govinda explains as follows the mandala symbolism of an image showing the Buddha in a stupa surrounded by a circle:

> The pilgrim sees the image of the Perfected One in a stupa, which has arisen in his own inner consciousness, as living reality filling its form: for the enlightened, perfected human being, that is, the one who has become a complete human being, is not only a replica of the universe but its coming to consciousness.[22]

The tension of masculine and feminine reflects a polarity at the heart of the real which has always haunted the human mind. Characteristic of Tantric Buddhism is that the integration or overcoming of this polarity is sought at once on the physical and the mental plane. On the mental plane the matrix world symbolizes the passive aspect, what is known, while the diamond world symbolizes the active principle, the knower. The one who has been initiated by the guru in an elaborate ritual understands the symbolic language, penetrates the circles of the mandala, completes the reunification of the separated poles, attains Buddhahood, and acquires magic powers (Sanskrit: *siddhi*). The totality of human being is realized in the "three secrets" of body, mouth, and mind, manifested in gestures (mudrā), speech (mantra) and enlightened will (bodhicitta), which connect the human microcosm with the universal cosmic Buddha.

The mantra, a sacred expression carrying mysterious power, is an essential element of Tantric initiation, conferring on the recipient higher powers which can henceforth be aroused anew and increased every time the initiate recites the magical syllables entrusted to him. The meditative function of the mantra comes in second place, but is scarcely less important. In the mantras the recurring syllable *Aum,* which begins with the primordial sound *A,* is the highest expression of the diamond world, while the equally frequent syllable *Namu* signifies the matrix world. The famous mantra of the beloved bodhisattva Avalokiteśvara (Kannon), *Aum maṇi padme hum,* referring to the jewel in the lotus, has been called "the eternal melody of Tibet" (Lama Govinda); in its constant repetition it becomes a form of meditation.

The importance of meditation is forcefully stressed by Kūkai, who sees it as the royal road to "attaining enlightenment in this very existence" ("becoming a Buddha in this body," Japanese: *sokushin jōbutsu*), an idea already approximated in Theravāda meditation which aims at "nirvāṇa here and now" (*diṭṭhadhama-nibbāna*):

> From the endless cycle of saṃsāra how can we be freed?
> The only way is to practice meditation and correct thinking.
> The samādhi of Prajñā is expounded by the Buddha himself;
> May His mercy be poured on me who am about to interpret it.[23]

The Buddha referred to here is Mahāvairocana, identical with the cosmic dharmakāya. Through meditation we awaken to our unity with this ultimate reality:

> If a student of samādhi enters the meditation called the "observation of Suchness, the Dharmakāya," he will have a vision that all is undifferentiated oneness like infinite space. If he concentrates on practicing this meditation continually, he will in his present life

> enter the first stage of Bodhisattvahood and quickly accumulate the merits and provisions which would otherwise take immeasurable aeons. Being embraced by the grace of all the Tathāgatas, he will reach the final stage and be equipped with the all-embracing wisdom; then, he will realize the unity of himself and others and be integrated in the Dharmakāya of all the Tathāgatas. With the great compassion that pours forth unconditionally, he will benefit endless sentient beings and thus engage in the great activities of the Buddha.[24]

Pure Land

Does meditation enjoy the same prominence in Amida Buddhism as in the other branches of Mahāyāna? The question is natural in view of the devotional nature of the Amida cult and the development of religious praxis in this tradition. The pious believer in Amida is more inclined to develop attitudes of marveling praise and trustful surrender than an inner-directed meditation. Yet in the wide sense meditation has an important place in the Pure Land schools.

In the great system of Chih-i, meditation and Pure Land devotion belong to different categories, the former being based on Self Power and leading to an experience of enlightenment. There is a meditative practice in Pure Land Buddhism, but it is oriented to seeing the form of Amida Buddha and his Western Paradise. "Throughout all Pure Land Scriptures of India, meditation upon Amitābha Buddha (*buddhānusmṛti*) was the essential practice."[25] This meditative nembutsu refers back to a ceremony in remembrance of the Buddha Śākyamuni, which the community practiced even in his lifetime, and which is known as buddhānusmṛti, the precise Sanskrit equivalent of nembutsu. *Smṛti* is also the equivalent of the Pali "sati," which we have met earlier in the sense of the "mindfulness" of Theravāda meditation. Instead of Śākyamuni, it is Amida Buddha that is now invoked. Meditative nembutsu is known as "vision of the Buddha" (Japanese: *kambutsu*), a phrase occurring in the

Chinese title of the *Meditation Sūtra.* Here is an example of the numerous visualization techniques recommended by this sutra:

> In order to perceive the Buddha of Immeasurable Life, begin with one of the physical features; that is, you should perceive just the twist of white hair between his eyebrows until it becomes very clear and distinct. Once you have seen the twist of white hair between his eyebrows, the eighty-four thousand features appear of their own accord. Once you have seen the Buddha of Immeasurable Life, you see at once the countless buddhas of the ten quarters.[26]

Hui-yüan's White Lotus assemblies, which brought this meditation to China, ardently sought after visions of Amida Buddha, in the spirit of several other texts of this time which taught methods of visualizing Buddhas and bodhisattvas. From the fifth century, meditative nembutsu penetrated deep into folk piety, and it is still widely practiced throughout East Asia.

Meditative nembutsu is distinguished from the recitation of the Buddha's name that relies on the saving action of Other Power. As the school developed, a combination of meditative and recitative nembutsu was practiced, the latter gaining more and more in strength until it completely overwhelmed the former. The scriptural basis for recitative nembutsu is found in texts such as the account of Amida Buddha's eighteenth vow in the *Larger Pure Land Sūtra:*

> If, after I have attained Buddhahood, the sentient beings in the ten quarters, who have Sincere Mind, Serene Faith, and Desire to be born in my country, should not be born, even with ten thoughts (utterances), may I not attain the Perfect Enlightenment.[27]

The words "even with ten thoughts" lend themselves to different interpretations. Certainly thoughts about the Buddha Amida are meant. But the thoughts, expressed in words, may be understood more generally as invocations of the Buddha. Thus the vow can be taken to prescribe not only meditative remembrance of the Buddha but the utterance of his name. This interpretation is reinforced by two other texts in which the reference to the name of Amida is explicit. In the *Smaller Pure Land Sūtra* we read:

> If one, hearing of Amida Buddha, bears the name in mind for one day, two days . . . or seven days with the thought undisturbed, one will see Amida at one's death bed and obtain Birth.[28]

The specification of the number "ten" in the eighteenth vow seems to urge repetition of the name. The *Meditation Sūtra,* the most important for our topic, after having expounded fifteen kinds of lofty meditative practice, goes on to teach a practice whereby those of lesser talent and sinners can be saved:

> When the life of such a foolish person is about to end, he meets a virtuous and learned teacher who comforts him in various ways, expounds for him the exquisite teachings, and urges him to be mindful of the Buddha. But this person is too tormented by pain to be mindful of the Buddha. Then the virtuous friend says, "If you cannot be mindful of the Buddha, you should say that you take refuge in the Buddha of Immeasurable Life." And so, with a sincere mind and an uninterrupted voice, this person says "Namu Amida Butsu" manifesting ten moments of thought; and because he says the Buddha's name, with every thought-moment, the evil karma binding him to birth-and-death for eighty *koṭis* is eliminated.[29]

Here the ten thoughts are explicitly connected with the tenfold invocation. This easy path opens salvation to the great mass of common, sinful people; for them, in this degenerate final age of the Latter Days of the Law, reciting the nembutsu is the only way of escape.

The process by which the recitative nembutsu supplanted the meditative variety can be traced in the first three patriarchs of the Chinese Pure Land school. T'an-luan, the first patriarch, practiced recitative nembutsu. He was concerned about the salvation of common people and took refuge in Other Power. Yet he admitted the validity of other practices, and wavered in his interpretation of the "ten thoughts" in the eighteenth vow. His successor Tao-ch'o emphasized the theme of the Latter Days of the Law, and he distinguished the "holy path" open only to great saints from the path of the Pure Land, easily accessible to all through nembutsu recitation. He was ardent in recommending the invocation of the name, though he does not use the term "nembutsu" exclusively in this sense:

> If we utter the Name even once, we are able to get rid of the sins of Birth-and-Death of eight thousand million kalpas. Even one utterance bears this fruit. How much more with continual utterance![30]

The third patriarch, Shan-tao, composed an extensive literary oeuvre, culminating in a four-volume commentary on the *Meditation Sūtra,* which is the definitive presentation of the nembutsu in the Chinese language. He finds both the meditative and the recitative nembutsu in the sūtra, but sees the highest form of Amida devotion in the invocation of Amida's name presented at the end of the sūtra. Even the less gifted, who are incapable of intensive mental concentration, can surely attain birth in the Pure Land by this practice. The other forms of meditation taught by the sūtra, on the form, the body, and the Pure Land of the Buddha, are valuable for the talented and advanced. But "the purpose is, if viewed from the intention of the Buddha's Vow, to make all beings single-heartedly and exclusively utter Amida's name."[31] Thus the invocation of the Name is not only the high point of Pure Land meditation, but claims exclusive status. The practice, like all forms of Pure Land piety, is based on deep faith in Amida's vows, and it is the most effective expression of this faith, for the invocation of Amida is the "rightly determining action for Birth." Hence the extraordinary zeal with which Shan-tao practices the nembutsu himself and spurs his disciples to do the same. "Whether walking, standing, sitting or lying, regardless of the length of time, hold it without any break of time."[32]

Hōnen, the founder of the Japanese Pure Land (Jōdo) school, followed in Shan-tao's footsteps. Devotion to Amida, propagated by the Tendai school, had entrenched itself in Japanese Buddhist piety long before his time. Genshin (942–1017), author of the much-read *Essential Passages on Birth in the Pure Land* (*Ōjōyōshū*), had given pre-eminence to the meditative nembutsu. Hōnen was converted to the nembutsu during his intensive study of Shan-tao's commentary on the *Meditation Sūtra*. In his *Selection of Passages on the Original Vow* (*Senchakushū,* 1198), the foundational text of the Pure Land sect, he declared that all forms of mixed practice must be relinquished in favor of the exclusive recitation of the Name, not only because of the weakness of people in this degenerate age, which makes the holy path impossible, but also because the nembutsu excels all other practices and "embodies all kinds of virtue."[33] He abandoned the practice of visualization: "Even if spiritual novices are successful in creating a vision of Amida," he declared, "in beauty it will never rival the carvings of the great masters, nor could a vision of the Pure Land be as lovely as the real flowers of the cherry, plum, peach or pear."[34] In his dedication to reciting the Name, Hōnen aimed at amazing achievements in daily practice. Shan-tao did not give figures when he urged the constant recitation of Namu Amida Butsu, but we know that Hōnen was soon reciting it sixty thousand times a day, and seventy thousand times in the final years of his life. Artistic representations show him with a string of pearls in his hand, a kind of rosary. These saints of the nembutsu were penetrated by and enwrapped in the Holy Name.

There are analogies with the story of the Russian pilgrim who is taught by a *staretz* (spiritual guide) to recite the name of Jesus, first three thousand times a day, then six thousand times, and later twelve thousand times until he is exhausted. The staretz, following the Slavonic *Philocalia* (1793), recommends the pilgrim to sit still in solitude, with bowed head and closed eyes, breathing softly, and looking into his heart; then to bring his thinking down from the head to the heart, and to repeat, either with the lips or only mentally: "Lord Jesus Christ, have mercy on me." All intruding thoughts are to be put aside while he persists quietly with this invocation, in stillness.[35] It is clear that recitation here is intended to lead into meditation. In the cases both of the Jesus prayer and the nembutsu, spiritual wisdom can be discerned behind the prescription of a daunting number of recitals. Repetition of the word lets its content sink deeper than the conscious level; thought descends into the heart—thus the prayer the pilgrim learns is also known as the heart prayer. The parallels between Jesus prayer and nembutsu go beyond the psychology of meditation to a common structure of faith, confident hope of salvation, and trust in infinite mercy.

The Way of Zen

The reader will have been struck by the contrast between the unadorned spareness of early Buddhist meditation and the lively meditation rituals of Mahāyāna. But in these too, and especially in Zen, the most important Buddhist way of meditation, the features of mindfulness and bodiliness are prominent. These features confer a striking modernity on Zen.

Within the wide spectrum of Buddhist meditation the Zen school took distinct form in China from the sixth century, showing the influence of the indigenous Taoist tradition, and it eventually spread beyond China to the whole of East Asia (Korea, Japan, and also Vietnam). The Bodhidharma legends tell of its origins. It flourished greatly during the second half of the T'ang dynasty (eighth and ninth centuries) and the Northern Sung dynasty (960–1127), as an extensive literature testifies.

Zen roots the spiritual life in the clear-sighted perception of everyday realities. Seeing things as they are, in their dependent co-origination, in their emptiness, the Zen practitioner attains a first-hand grasp of Buddhist wisdom and becomes independent of texts and conceptual systems. The confidence of this tradition is exuberantly expressed in the teaching styles of the T'ang-dynasty masters: Ma-tsu (709–88), Pai-chang (720–814), Huang-po (d. 850) and Lin-chi, four generations related by "a direct transmission from mind to mind." These masters draw on the common language of the Chinese people, eschewing technical terms deriving from the Indian sources. Though there is far more scholarship and speculation in the background than is often imagined, the figure who comes to prominence here is not the scholar or the philosopher but Lin-chi's "common person of no rank," a human being awake to reality and freed of the delusions of habitual perception.

Of course the tradition could not remain at this high peak of vitality forever. An institutionalization of Ch'an teaching and practice was inevitable. The dazzling kōans were systematized and adjusted to the stages of a disciple's development, notably by the Japanese Zen Master Hakuin. The practical aspects of meditation were fixed at an early date in the manual *Tso-ch'an i* by Tsung-tse (or Tsung-i) of the Yün-men lineage. Following this text, Dōgen (1200–1253), the founder of the Sōtō school in Japan, composed the oldest Japanese handbook of Zen meditation, the *General Teachings for the Promotion of Zazen* (*Fukan Zazengi*), which gives the basic directions followed in Japan to the present day.[36] He wrote the first version of this, his earliest work, in fewer than a thousand Chinese characters, immediately after his return from China in 1227, where he had for five years dedicated himself with intense effort to meditation.

The manual begins with an exhortation to the practice of meditation in the erect *zazen* position in which the dharma or the Tao, that is, the complete enlightenment of all Buddhas and Patriarchs, will be attained. It points to the example of Śākyamuni, who, according to Zen tradition, sat erect in meditation for six years before the eye of wisdom opened itself for him in enlightenment. The image of Bodhidharma, whose nine years gazing at a wall was a prized legacy of the Zen school, provides another spur to practice. Dōgen urges quick commitment to actual performance and provides instructions for it:

> For sanzen [= zazen], a quiet room is suitable. Eat and drink moderately. Cast aside all involvements and cease all affairs. Do not think good or bad. Do not administer pros and cons. Cease all the movements of the conscious mind, the gauging of all thoughts and views. Have no designs on becoming a Buddha. [Sanzen] has nothing whatever to do with sitting or lying down.[37]

The last two sentences, not found in the 1233 version, are ideas of great moment to Dōgen. The following section with its precise descriptions of the bodily posture of sitting erect is the center of the manual. The significance of breathing is emphasized in the closing sentences, which form a transition to the account of the mental disposition to be maintained:

> Once you have adjusted your posture, take a deep breath, inhale and exhale, rock your body right and left into a steady, immobile sitting position. Think of not-thinking. How do you think of not-thinking? Non-thinking. This in itself is the essential art of zazen.[38]

The three central sections of the manual present erect zazen as "the Dharma gate of repose and bliss." Though evidently related to the Yoga tradition, zazen goes beyond it in essential ways. In Dōgen's understanding, it is more than a mere exercise of concentration or a precondition for experience; it is itself the experience, enacting the nonduality of mind and body which is a defining trait of Dōgen's metaphysical outlook. Zazen embraces one's own enlightenment and the enlightenment of all living beings. Buddhas sitting in zazen possess the fulfillment of salvation. Dōgen set forth the significance of the body for meditation both in his instructions for practice and in his doctrinal remarks. "The attainment of the Way is truly accomplished with the body."[39] Persuaded of the all-importance of the body he tirelessly urged his disciples to sit.

What then is the significance of the famous motto, "drop off body and mind," which Dōgen claimed to have learned from his Chinese master Ju-ching (1163–1228)? It is to be taken as a call to radical detachment. One casts aside all concern with self, with past or future, with physical discomfort or emotional moods, and throws oneself body and mind into the practice of the Buddha way in the here and now. This practice is an end in itself, not pursued for selfish aims. Thus one opens oneself to one's Buddha nature, the "selfless self" which is already, intrinsically enlightened.

It is hard to add new inflections to the overall image of Zen conveyed by the vast literature now available in Western languages, although one would like to see further research on particular points. The specific identity of the Zen way was captured by the T'ang masters in the famous lines, attributed to Bodhidharma:

A special transmission outside the scriptures,
Not founded upon words and letters;
By pointing directly to [one's] mind,
It lets one see into [one's own true] nature and [thus] attain Buddhahood.[40]

The masters' declaration of their independence from the scriptures, which in all other Buddhist schools enjoyed the highest esteem and were the normative authority, and their bold appeal to the authority of their own experience, did not keep them from being versed in the scriptural tradition and from using scriptural texts in guiding disciples to their own personal experience. Independence of letters is a spiritual attitude, as is seen from the vast literary production to which Zen gave rise, in the chronicles and kōan collections which are still serviceable in spiritual direction today. The essential thing is not to confuse the fingers that point at the moon with the actual reality, designated by the phrase "pointing to the human mind." This is uniquely and only a matter of the practitioner's personal experience.

Zen tradition strongly emphasizes the crucial importance of practice and experience. Thereby, the individual practitioner is thrust back on his or her own individual self. This is perhaps the reason why the tradition has produced so many unforgettable and inimitable personalities, many of whom were thrillingly sketched by the pen of D.T. Suzuki. Their luminous wisdom and generous warmth of heart have a particular impact in the darkness of our times.

The basic practices of Zen, sitting and breathing, are common Asian features. The kōan is something special, a product of the profound wit and unpredictable reactions of original Zen masters. The motive of doubt and searching is central to all Zen kōans and anecdotes. Wrestling with a kōan brings long periods of frustration and states of anguish until one achieves an experiential breakthrough. The Zen Buddhist explicates this experience in the sense of Mahāyāna doctrine. At this time of epochal convulsions and exciting paradigm shifts the Zen experience of self and of unity is highly valued. The physicist Carl Friedrich von Weizsäcker believes that the overcoming of Cartesian and Newtonian dualism and the challenges of Eastern spirituality will give rise to a new integrated consciousness. He sees Zen as playing a crucial role in this. Certainly, the simple human quality of the basic Zen exercises allows them to be adopted by all those who are seeking a richer experience of self and cosmos today.

Western Responses to Buddhist Meditation

Modern urban and technological culture has brought with it a great amount of frenzy and stress, which has made the culture of meditation not only deeply attractive to many Westerners, but an indispensable remedy to the ills that press on humankind. The practical advice about the cultivation of mindfulness that can be found in Western monastic traditions and spiritual writers is enhanced by the new input from the East, distinguished by its concreteness and easy applicability.

One example of this cross-fertilization is the method of the Indian Jesuit Anthony de Mello, who has developed a Christian *sadhana* meditation based on the principle of mindfulness, which borrows from satipaṭṭhāna meditation.[41] Starting from the high value of silence, without which no meditation is possible ("Modern man is unfortunately plagued by a nervous tension that makes it almost impossible for him to be quiet"[42]), De Mello has his students practice mere awareness (sati). "Don't seek for anything sensational in the revelation that silence brings. In fact don't seek at all. Limit yourself to observing. Just take in everything that comes to your awareness."[43] If they practice this observing persistently they are sure to realize the usefulness of their effort, indicated in mental habits of stillness and concentration.

De Mello leads his students to pure awareness in the style of the satipaṭṭhāna method:

> Suppose you choose breathing as your basic object of attention. Then your exercise will possibly go something like this—"I am breathing. . . . I am breathing. . . ." and in an extension of this awareness: "Now I am thinking. . . . thinking. . . . thinking. . . . Now I am listening to a sound. . . . listening. . . . listening. . . ."[44]

The great value of this exercise is that it brings about a psychic change in an apparently effortless way. De Mello links mindfulness to the involvement of the body. He teaches an exercise on body sensations in which one is to become aware of the body in each of its limbs. Complete awareness, he says, also brings relaxation. The important thing is that the practitioners overcome headiness and withdraw their attention from the realm of thinking and speaking to that of feeling, sensing, loving, intuiting. Body prayer, in which the appropriate gestures are performed, gives power and body to prayer and leads on to higher levels.

The Western reception of Zen has given rise to a reception of Zen meditation by Christian meditation masters. Two of my Jesuit colleagues in Japan have been to the fore in bringing this spirituality to the West. Hugo M. Enomiya-Lassalle, who became a Japanese citizen and also an honorary citizen of Hiroshima as an outstanding victim of the atom bomb, made Zen his own as few non-Asians have managed to do. His book *Zen Meditation for Christians* can be used as a practical manual for meditation. Here he emphasizes the bodily postures prescribed by Zen (following the *Fukan Zazengi*). Even if the posture is painful or difficult at the start, if one carries on with it correctly "it causes no tension in the body, which should be completely relaxed." Zen practice aims at having the body experience calm. The mental disposition of *munen musō* (without concepts and without images) is the one of meditation without object practiced by many great Christian mystics.[45]

J.L. Kadowaki, who like Enomiya-Lassalle has mastered Zen meditation and uses it for Christian spirituality, shows in his book *Zen and the Bible* the significance of the body for a deeply experiental reading of

Holy Scripture. Dōgen's saying, "Each and every line of the sūtras is the living body-mind of the Buddha and the Patriarchs" inspired him to practice what he calls "body-reading." This reading with complete dedication of body and mind leads to an integral understanding of religious writings. "When I started to practice Zen and came to understand the words of Dōgen mentioned above, my method of reading the Bible changed completely."[46]

The complementarity between Christian prayer and Buddhist meditation has been explored by many others, beginning with Friedrich Heiler, who contrasted "Buddha, the master of concentration" and "Jesus, the master of prayer." Meditation and prayer, far from being mutually exclusive, stand in a polar relationship to one another. If a totally secularized person practices meditation without any prayer, putting it on the same level as the use of drugs, the result is that the integrity of meditation itself is undermined by the lopping off of its transcendent dimension. Christian meditation is rooted in hearing the biblical Word and in prayerful communal worship. The appropriation of the meditative wisdom of Buddhism can deepen and illuminate this biblical and liturgical practice.

VI

Transcendence and the Absolute

The Buddhist tradition has shown itself reserved toward metaphysical speculation. This is especially the case in the early period. The silence of Śākyamuni about metaphysical questions, which we have already referred to in connection with the ultimate reality of the self, inaugurated an attitude of prudence. Later forms of Theravāda and especially of Mahāyāna Buddhism developed elaborate philosophical systems, but these remain rooted in the original Buddhism of Śākyamuni, and share his distaste for inquiries that are not concerned with the path of liberation. It would, however, be wrong to conclude from this that Buddhists ever refrained from the search for transcendence, or that they never attained an experiential grasp of transcendent reality. The Buddhist sense of the transcendent has not, to be sure, been put in the foreground as something easily communicated. To bring it to light we must bring a discerning empathy to the sources, and examine them with close attention.

If we do so, we shall find that the theme of transcendence emerges in Buddhism in a rich variety of forms. There are many affirmative, richly eloquent celebrations of the supreme reality, but it is more characteristic of the tradition to use negation as a cipher of the transcendent. The three most prominent forms of such a use of negation in world religions are: falling silent before the mystery, speaking of ineffability, and naming the mystery directly with negative titles. We find these modes of negation both in Buddhism and Christianity, though in such different guises that the gulf between Buddhist and Christian "negative theology" is almost as great as that between the positive teachings of the two religions. Nevertheless, the shared sense of the radical inadequacy of all language before the ultimate creates a particularly strong sense of communion between the two traditions at this point.

Since negative statements do not define their content, they lend themselves in many cases, indeed in almost all cases, to a variety of interpretations. This variety has been particularly evident in Buddhism. It makes the task of discerning the theme of transcendence in these negative statements all the more complex, and all the more necessary. We must bear in mind, too, that none of the statements can be studied in abstraction from the concrete doctrinal context to which it refers.

The Silence of the Buddha

The silence of the historical Buddha Śākyamuni can be seen as the first expression of negative theology in Buddhism. This silence is a prominent mark of the Buddha's career, continuing through the entire forty-five years of his teaching, and becoming an explicit theme whenever metaphysical questions are put to him and he answers by remaining silent. Such questions are: "Is the world eternal or not? Has the world an end or not? Is the soul the same as the body or different? Does the Tathāgata, the Perfected One, exist after his death or not?" These are questions that concern the ultimate nature of reality. The question about the post-mortem state of the Tathāgata touches on the topic of nirvāna, which in primitive Buddhism is conceived as the state of the highest self-actualization of the Tathāgata. The Buddha's silence suggests that the questions are basically misplaced, and lead to that entanglement in views against which the Buddha frequently warns:

> Attachment to teachings leads to discussion.
> How, by what means to discuss the man without attachment?
> He takes up and rejects nothing—
> He has washed away all views here. (*Suttanipāta* 787)[1]

The Pali Canon has transmitted a conversation between the disciple Mālunkyāputta and the Buddha. In response to the disciple's eager questioning on the above-mentioned metaphysical topics, the Buddha says:

> Did I ever speak thus to you, Mālunkyāputta: "Come you, Mālunkyāputta, fare the Brahma-faring under me and I will explain to you either that the world is eternal or that the world is not eternal . . . or that the Tathāgata neither is nor is not after dying?". . . Mālunkyāputta, it is as if a man were pierced by an arrow that was thickly smeared with poison and his friends and relations, his kith and kin, were to procure a physician and surgeon. He might speak thus: "I will not draw out this arrow until I know of the man who pierced me whether he is a noble or brahman or merchant or worker. . . . I will not draw out this arrow until I know of the shaft by which I was pierced whether it was of reeds of this kind or that. . . .[2]

and so on through a list of otiose inquiries. The all-important message of release from suffering is ignored, while the mind wrestles with insoluble riddles. The Buddha is often compared with a physician in the Buddhist literature, and his silence is explained as a pragmatic and pedagogic one; he refuses to let his salvific role be obscured by the distraction of mere knowledge, however wise or deep; when one is rescuing someone from a burning house, one does not use the occasion to give the rescuee a tutorial in philosophy.

This explanation of the Buddha's silence as prompted by consideration for the hearer has a salutary point, in that it warns us against the temptation to escape from the concrete problem of existence into unreal speculation. But there is a deeper aspect to the Buddha's silence: it is silence before unfathomable, ineffable mystery. Another dialogue in the Pali Canon, this time between King Pasenadi of Kosala and the wise nun Khemā, proceeds at first in much the same way as the dialogue with Mālunkyāputta. Then, when the king asks the reason for the Buddha's silence, Khemā asks whether the king has a reckoner who could number the sands of the Ganges or the drops of the ocean. No, and why not? Because the great ocean is deep, unmeasurable, unfathomable, and so, too, is the nature of the Perfected One. If one says of it that "it exists," this does not apply; "it does not exist" does not apply, "it both exists and does not exist" does not apply, "it neither exists nor does not exist" does not apply.

These statements sound quite like the refrain of the sage Yājña-valkya in one of the oldest *Upanishads:* "The self is not this, not this (*neti, neti*). He is incomprehensible for he is never comprehended."[3] The origins of this negative theology can be traced back to the hymns of the *Vedas:* "Outside and within all beings is he; he moves and he moves not; because of his subtlety, incomprehensible; far, but yet near. . . . Loftier even than the lofty Gāyatri, beyond the Immortal he strode forth. Where was the Unborn then? This even the knowers of Vedic lore cannot tell."[4] The gesture of negation—*neti, neti*—points to the ultimate that lies beyond all human concepts.

Another dialogue, between the Buddha and the wanderer Vaccha-gotta, confirms that his silence is not merely pedagogic but points to an unfathomable mystery. Frustrated by the ineffability of the Tathāgata's mode of being, the disciple exclaims:

> "I am at a loss on this point, good Gotama, I am bewildered, and that measure of satisfaction I had from former conversation with the good Gotama—even that have I now lost."
>
> "You ought to be at a loss, Vaccha, you ought to be bewildered. For, Vaccha, this dhamma is deep, difficult to see, difficult to understand, peaceful, excellent, beyond dialectic, subtle, intelligible to the wise. . . . If someone were to question you thus, Vaccha: 'That fire that was in front of you and that has been

> quenched—to which direction has that fire gone from here?' . . . What would you reply?"
>
> "It does not apply, good Gotama. For, good Gotama, that fire blazed because of a supply of grass and sticks, yet from having totally consumed this and from the lack of other fuel, being without fuel it is reckoned to be quenched."
>
> "Even so, Vaccha, that material shape by which one recognizing the Tathāgata might recognize him—that material shape has been got rid of by the Tathāgata, cut off at the root, made like a palm-tree stump that can come to no further existence and is not liable to arise again in the future. . . ."[5]

and so on through each of the five skandhas.

The Buddha's silence has been taken as an agnostic gesture, or as suggesting that the nirvanic state is one of blank annihilation. It seems clear that it was not any uncertainty that sealed the Buddha's lips, but a sense of ineffable mystery. In the primitive Buddhist conception, nirvāṇa, which literally means "extinguishing," and is thus a negative expression, evoking associations of "nothing" or "nonbeing," nonetheless also carries overtones of transcendence. As we argued in chapter two, the nihilistic interpretation must be rejected, for it cannot do justice to the phenomenology of a reality which attracts such titles as "haven of refuge," "island in the flood," "place of bliss," "remedy for all ill," "the state of him who is worthy (the arhat)." Nakamura is one of many scholars who insist that the negative declarations have to be taken as constituting something like a negative theology:

> It is true that the Buddha tried to refuse replying to the question of the ultimate reality which lay beyond the categories of the phenomenal world, but he did not seem to have had any doubts about the absolute. He said: "There is an unborn, an unoriginated, an unmade, an uncompounded; were there not, there would be no escape from the world of the born, the originated, the made, and the compounded" (*Udāna* VIII 3). The Buddha thus believed in something that remains latently beneath the shifting appearances of the visible world.[6]

Similar remarks apply to such thinkers as Nāgārjuna, whom we shall meet shortly. The nihilistic interpretation is a facile one, and betrays deafness to the serene and joyful tone of the texts, which has caused them to be preserved as sources of religious enlightenment.

Early Buddhist negative theology possesses an astonishing wealth of powerful statements. We cannot follow the further development of this strand in the tradition in detail. There were some deviations in a nihilistic direction in Theravāda Buddhism, but nothing of the sort is apparent at the level of popular religion, where the sense of transcendence found mythic and legendary expression in new religious ideas and rituals.

The Way of Negation

The Mahāyāna movement brought the richest unfolding of the Buddhist sense of transcendence. The great Mahāyāna sūtras, especially the *Perfection of Wisdom* sūtras, develop the way of negation, crystallized in the powerful formulations of the Indian Nāgārjuna, the most influential and perhaps the greatest Buddhist philosopher.[7] In the second century he developed his philosophy of the Middle Path (Mādhyamika) in dependence on the *Perfection of Wisdom* literature and its vision of emptiness.[8] His creative genius may have even played some role in the formation of this literature.

The interpretation of Nāgārjuna's terse and cryptic texts is one of the storm centers of Buddhist thought, and has become a preoccupation of Western scholars and philosophers in recent decades. No other thinker has pursued negation with such consequent radicality. As a result, his thought has often been classified as nihilist by Western scholars, an interpretation that can be refuted from Nāgārjuna's own statements and that is generally regarded as untenable today. Neither can his negation be explained from the undeniably dialectical character of his thinking. A text attributed to Nāgārjuna, the *Mahāyānaviṃśikā,* opens with praise of the Buddha "who has presented the doctrine that cannot be expressed by words," suggesting that the Mādhyamika practice of negation is motivated by concerns similar to those of negative theology. Nāgārjuna says expressly that emptiness (śūnyatā) does not signify annihilation, and he lists ten attributes of emptiness that unmistakably have positive connotations: emptiness is unhindered, omnipresent, without differentiations, wide open, without appearance, spotlessly pure, unmoved (without coming to be or passing away), without being, empty of emptiness, and without possessions. Similar lists can be found in the wisdom sūtras. The way the tradition relativizes even its own most refined utterances (classed as conventional truth), as well as its insistence on the emptiness of emptiness itself, give eloquent testimony to its sense of an absolute reality.

Nāgārjuna's emptiness philosophy has its point of origin in the original basic Buddhist teachings of non-self and dependent origination which, when worked out consequently, lead to a radical relativization of all existing things. Since there is no entity (dharma) that has not come into existence in dependent origination, every entity is lacking in proper nature (own being), or is empty (śūnya). Emptiness is thus implicit in dependent origination; to name one is to name the other. "Dependent origination, that we name emptiness" declares Nāgārjuna in a strophe of the *Verses on the Middle Way* (*Mādhyamika-kārikā* 24,18). He develops the way of negation in the famous tetralemma, the four alternatives of affirmation (being), negation (nonbeing), double affirmation (both being and nonbeing), double negation (neither being nor nonbeing), through which he operates a reductio ad absurdum of all conceivable statements, refutes all fixed positions, and indicates the middle way between being and nonbeing. This middle lies beyond all four statement patterns and is, as Murti says, "beyond concepts and speech; it is transcendental, being a review of all things."[9] A positive grasp of the ultimate nature of things is simply impossible. "Like nirvāṇa, the true nature of things lies outside the realm of human knowing and cannot be grasped in words."[10]

As Candrakīrti, (seventh century CE), the next great thinker in the

Mādhyamika lineage, explains in the *Prasannapadā,* a classic commentary which clarifies Nāgārjuna's thought within Buddhist tradition, emptiness has a liberating function on the Buddhist path of salvation. "All worldly ideas are stopped without exception in emptiness, where there is a vision of the emptiness of the own being of all existents." To realize this emptiness of own being (svabhāva) leads to release from bondage. Not only the ego, as in early Buddhist teaching, but all things lack own being and are empty. The advance of the Mahāyāna doctrine consists in extending the notion of emptiness to the whole world of becoming. Emptiness causes all discursive thought, and the impurities associated with it, to disappear. "Hence one calls emptiness Nirvāṇa, as it brings to rest all discursive ideas." The world of becoming (saṃsāra) and nirvāṇa are both empty, and so there is no difference between them. The teaching of the Perfect One "aims at leading us to true reality," which is not dependent on anything else, calm, unimpeded by discursive ideas," and in which all discriminations are suppressed.[11]

Nāgārjuna and Candrakīrti describe true reality with negative words. Expressions which are equivalents of emptiness, for example, Suchness (tathatā) or the element of Dharma (dharmadhātu, dharmatā), are also clarified through negations. All of these expressions designate the unconditioned, or what we call the absolute, which is also, linguistically, a negative expression, as seen from its dictionary equivalents: independent, unrestricted, unconditional. The most positive name for ultimate reality in Nāgārjuna is *paramārtha-satya,* which is contrasted to the provisional reality of the world of becoming, *saṃvṛti-satya;* the contrast between the two is the doctrine of the twofold truth which we met in the course of our discussion of Chih-i. The ineffable highest truth is apprehended only by prajñā (wisdom).

A satisfactory interpretation of the emptiness philosophy of Nāgārjuna's Middle Way can never be attained by abstract philosophical categories. If we follow the Buddhist tradition, which esteems Nāgārjuna as a religious thinker of high rank, we begin to see him as close to the world of the *theologia negativa* developed in Neo-Platonism and given its first great Christian form in Pseudo-Dionysius, who sees the divine nature as wrapped in darkness, which the human mind can penetrate only "through the negation of vision and knowledge" (*De mystica theologia,* chapter two). Thus Nāgārjuna might be seen as a neighbor of the great Christian mystics of the patristic and medieval periods, even though the identity he discerns between nirvāṇa and saṃsāra is very remote from the Platonic form of thought that has been so influential in the West.[12] A modern poet, T.S. Eliot, plays on the deep meaning of negation in his *Four Quartets:* "I said to my soul, be still, and let the dark come upon you / Which shall be the darkness of God" (*East Coker*). The eye of wisdom can discern in Nāgārjuna's darkness the light that shines on the negative path.

The Cosmic Dimension

In contrast to the radicality of Nāgārjuna's Mādhyamika school—which strives through negation to overcome all contraries of yes and no, being and nonbeing, vacuity and fullness, reaching for an unattainable ultimate—the second great Mahāyāna philosophy, the Vijñānavāda or School of Consciousness, seeks a more horizontal or cosmic expansion of vision. The school developed early on a doctrine of consciousness of considerable metaphysical and psychological depth. The storehouse consciousness (*ālaya-vijñāna*), the central notion in the thought of the school, is as absolute consciousness essentially identical with the suchness (tathatā) of the Buddha nature and with the cosmic Buddha body (dharmakāya). It contains immaculate, original seeds (*bīja*) as well as defiled karmic ones which produce manifestations in the world of becoming. The school developed the theory of eight consciousnesses (the five sense consciousnesses, mind, the thinking consciousness, and the storehouse consciousness) so influential in Buddhist psychology. The immaculate seed of the Buddha matrix ripens in a ninth immaculate consciousness (*amala-vijñāna*). Two favorites metaphors in Mahāyāna writing clarify the relation of the provisional, unreal appearances to the absolute. The seeds are compared to waves which do not exist in separation from the ocean out of which they seem to emerge, but in which all waters are contained. Or the immaculate seed, as Buddha matrix and potential Buddha nature, belongs to the absolute realm as a hidden treasure or jewel, which is covered with the dirt of the world of becoming and which is to be discovered in enlightenment.

The countless seeds brought forth by the storehouse consciousness permit a world of appearances to arise, which in a process of development return to their origin in the fundamental consciousness. Thus the world of becoming, unmasked as empty, is philosophically clarified in its emergence from and reversion to mind or consciousness, the only reality (Sanskrit: *citta mātra,* or mind only). Since the school is concerned with realizing this vision, its presentations are of importance for meditation. This aspect is apparent in another of the school's titles, Yogācāra or "the practice of yoga."

The great Yogācāra teacher Asaṅga (290–360) brought the doctrine of the three bodies (*trikāya*) to its perfect shape in his tract *Mahāyāna-saṃgraha,* mapping a path from the body of appearance (nirmāṇakāya) via the reward body (sambhogakāya) to the dharma body (dharmakāya), also called the cosmic body, since it fills and penetrates the cosmos. The dharma body, as the essence of Buddhahood, is common to all Buddhas and transcends their multiplicity as the core principle of the process that leads one to final enlightenment. This key idea goes back to early Buddhism:

> Do not wail, saying "Our teacher has passed away, and we have no one to follow." What I have taught, the Dharma with the vinaya (disciplinary) rules, will be your teacher after my departure. If you adhere to them and practice them uninterruptedly, is it not the same as if my Dharma body (dharmakāya) remained here forever?[13]

The Buddha is present in the dharma: "Who sees the Dharma, sees me" (*Itivuttaka* 92).[14]

The dharma body as the hidden principle of reality is beyond the grasp of our mind. The *Diamond Sūtra,* one of the *Perfection of Wisdom* scriptures, praises it in the following terms:

> The Lord:
> Those who by my form did see me,
> And those who followed me by my voice,
> Wrong are the efforts they engaged in,
> Me these people will not see.
> From the Dharma one should see the Buddha,
> For the Dharma-bodies are the guides.
> Yet Dharmahood is not something one should become aware of,
> Nor can one be made aware of it[15]

Vasubandhu, Asaṅga's younger brother and a chief representative of the Yogācāra school, speaks of the dharma body as "the blissful body of emancipation," "inconceivable, wholesome and stable."[16] Another text, the *Ratnagotravibhāga,* which belongs to the Tathāgatagarbha tradition (to be discussed shortly), speaks of the "depth" and "variety" of the dharma body, indicating by the word "variety" its cosmic dimension.[17]

The cosmic Buddha body became the central idea of the Chinese Nirvāṇa school, which was based on the *Nirvāṇa Sūtra* of the Mahāyāna (Sanskrit: *Mahāparinirvāṇa-sūtra*), and was later absorbed into T'ien-t'ai. The emergence of this school was preceded by the so-called *icchantika* controversy, which turned on the question whether the icchantika, described as "people given to sensual desires," could attain Buddhahood, as the esteemed monk Tao-sheng (ca.360–434) maintained. The issue was settled when the complete Chinese translation of the Mahāyāna *Nirvāṇa Sūtra* became known, for it declares that all sentient beings possess the Buddha nature. The Nirvāṇa school made itself the advocate of the two related teachings of universal Buddha nature and cosmic Buddha body. The possession of the Buddha nature was extended in the T'ien-t'ai school to all existing things, and the Buddha body was understood in equally comprehensive terms. In this view the cosmos as a whole and in all its parts is identical with the Buddha. The *Nirvāṇa Sūtra*'s doctrine that "All living beings possess the Buddha nature" is given a still wider scope by Zen master Dōgen who makes it read: "All beings are Buddha nature."

The Tathāgatagarbha thinkers (whose historical relation to the other schools is not easy to clarify) emphasize the proposition: "All living beings are possessed of the embryo of the Tathāgatha."[18] The matrix or embryo of the Tathāgata (Tathāgatagarbha) means the potential Buddha nature that pervades the whole of reality. The cognitive moment comes into effect especially in the process of ripening of this Buddha matrix.[19] This doctrine was to be one of the sources nourishing the Zen quest for the true self in its unity with the cosmos.

Cosmic Buddha body and universal Buddha nature are seen as formless and ineffable; they represent a transcendent reality, though one can hardly attribute to them an absolute transcendence in the sense of an essential difference in being that would put them beyond this world. To the Buddha nature are ascribed the attributes of permanence, blissfulness, suchness, and purity, which in their affirmative character seem to contrast with the philosophy of emptiness. This contrast did not prevent the Mādhyamika and Yogācāra schools from co-existing within Mahāyāna, for the idealist axiom of the latter, that all things are mind-only, together with its insistence on the insubstantiality of all things, preserved it from a realism incompatible with the emptiness philosophy.

Of greater interest to us than the philosophical consequences of the cosmic vision are its religious ones, which had such formative influence on the Mahāyāna tradition. The reverence which was first shown to the person of the Buddha was now transferred to the cosmos and all its parts, and the Buddha was found in every grain of rice. This attitude inspired a brief but precious chapter of Dōgen's *Shōbōgenzō,* titled "One Bright Pearl" (*Ikka Myōju*). Dōgen uses the pearl an an image of the Buddha nature hidden at the heart of things and unifying the cosmos:

> One bright pearl communicates directly through all time; being through all the past unexhausted, it arrives through all the present. While there is a body now, a mind now, they are the bright pearl.

> That stalk of grass, this tree, is not a stalk of grass, is not a tree; the mountains and rivers of this world are not the mountains and rivers of this world. They are the bright pearl.[20]

Some of the greatest Buddhist art reflects this sense of the Buddha's presence woven into the texture of the natural world, which could well serve, too, as an inspiration for contemporary environmental awareness.

The comprehensive sense of the cosmos in Mahāyāna corresponds to a deep need of our times. Since the encounter of Buddhism with Western science in the mid-nineteenth century, this special contribution of Buddhism to global culture has come prominently to the fore. Western science and technology have conquered the Asian world, but the West has also found there the necessary complement to its own one-sided rationality. Until the twentieth century, Asians related to the surrounding world with a sense of intimate proximity to nature, pervaded by religious associations. As technological civilization impinged on their lives, calling for an appropriate response from their religious traditions, Buddhism was able to invoke the scientificity it had cultivated in its centuries-long cognitive strivings. While Theravāda drew on the analytical Abhidharma philosophy for the intelligent appropriation of Western technology, Mahāyāna participated in the creation of a new, integrated view of the world, which chimed with the nondualist awareness of the unity and totality of the universe found in its sutras and philosophies.

In addition to the sources we have discussed, mention must be made of the *Avataṃsaka Sūtra* and the Hua-yen (Japanese: Kegon) philosophy which is based on it, and whose influence also pervades the Zen tradition. Hua-yen seems to anticipate in an extraordinary way the contemporary world picture. According to the wisdom of this school, the harmonious totality of the cosmos grows out of countless miniscule parts, grains of sand and drops of water, which in turn are each myriads of worlds in immeasurable spaces. The metaphors of mirrors which mirror and re-mirror each other to infinity and of the jewel net knit from thousands of precious stones express in overwhelming style the interrelatedness of all things in the universe. A similar thought was pursued by the great pioneer Teilhard de Chardin and in our days it has become a notion to which all sides make appeal. This convergence of Asian intellectuality and the postmodern world releases an age-old human longing to grasp the whole in its unity. Buddhism offers in symbolic form a world-formula embracing everything, which rather resembles the goal of the highest contemporary scientific ambition.[21]

Today the cosmic world picture of Buddhism must express itself in the ethical attitude of solidarity. Ethical consciousness of responsibility and fine esthetic sensitivity go hand in hand in the way the Japanese Buddhist avoids wasting a single grain of rice or drop of water. This attractive mentality, translated into contemporary terms, must show itself in action for the good of the environment. The urgent ecological problem, which has become a menace to the future of humanity, poses tasks which are no less pressing in Asia than in the West. No Eastern feeling for nature was able to prevent Japan from reaching in a few decades a fearful degree of pollution of the environment and destruction of nature. Other Asian countries have been quick to follow. This threatening situation summons the religions to make their contribution. During the last decades Buddhism has often manifested its readiness to cooperate in the service of the general welfare. In the endeavor to protect the world its motivation differs from the Christian one. While Christians speak mainly of "preserving the creation" and look to the Creator God, concerned engagement can also find a basis in the vision of the Buddha present in the cosmic whole.

Zen Enlightenment

Motifs of the emptiness and mind-only philosophies resonate in Zen teaching, not in any kind of theoretical synthesis but as practical resources to be drawn on in a free style. The negative way of the *Perfection of Wisdom* sūtras, the basic chord of Mahāyāna, is also what is most fundamental in Zen. But all the other Mahāyāna currents we have evoked above feed into the rich culture of Zen, though none of them have a formal, constraining authority over the Zen spiritual quest.

The first kōan of the *Wu-men kuan* (Japanese: *Mumonkan*) offers an initiation to the negative way. To a monk's question whether a dog has Buddha nature, Chao-chou answers "*Wu*"—no, nothing, or nothingness. It is clear that a direct way leads from emptiness, the center of Nāgārjuna's thought, to this Zen nothingness. The Zen school interpreted Nāgārjuna in this sense and saw themselves as his followers. Nothingness, like emptiness, is ineffable and is experienced in enlightenment.

The Vijñānavāda elements in Zen appear when the mental character of enlightenment is articulated. An exemplary instance is the twenty-ninth kōan of the *Wu-men kuan:*

> A temple flag was flapping in the wind, and two monks were having an argument about it. One said the flag was moving, the other that the wind was moving; and they could come to no agreement on the matter. The Patriarch said, "It is not that the wind is moving, it is not that the flag is moving; it is that your honorable minds are moving." The two monks were struck with awe.[22]

This episode illustrates the mind-only philosophy. But Zen masters do not rest content with this understanding; they see enlightenment in the awe that strikes the monks. In the enlightenment experience flag, wind, and mind are undifferentiatedly one: nothing and everything. This kōan eludes philosophical interpretation and points to the truth of ultimate reality that lies beyond all contraries. The same must be said of the central kōans of the collection, in which the emptiness philosophy is again blended with echoes of the mind-only philosophy:

> A monk asked Nan-chü'an, "Is there a truth which has not yet been explained?" Nan-chü'an replied, "There is." "What is this truth," said the monk, "which has so far not been explained? Nan-chü'an answered: "This is not mind; this is not Buddha; this is not a thing."
>
> Ta-mei asked Ma-tsu, "What is the Buddha?" Ma-tsu answered, "The mind is the Buddha."
>
> A monk asked Ma-tsu, "What is the Buddha?" Ma-tsu answered, "Neither the mind, nor the Buddha."[23]

The Zen capacity to integrate complex dialectics reminiscent of Nāgārjuna, metaphysical principles of cosmic Buddhahood, and a praxis directed to enlightenment is well illustrated in the "Buddha Nature" chapter of Dōgen's *Shōbōgenzō,* which moves from the thesis that "All sentient beings are Buddha nature," through the more profound thesis that "All sentient beings are not Buddha nature," to a vivid apprehension of the identity of Buddha nature and impermanence. In this apprehension all conceptual schemes fall away and the mind awakens to a coherent view of things which yet remains "as free and traceless as the flight of birds." "Do not vainly cherish life. Do not blindly dread death. They are where the Buddha nature is. Clinging in attachment to life, shrinking in abhorrence from death, is not Buddhist. Realizing that both life and death are a combination of various conditions being manifested before your eyes, you utilize a way of complete and unrestricted freedom."[24]

Zen enlightenment, as numerous accounts, both ancient and modern, make clear, is an experience of transcendence. D.T. Suzuki, referring to the expression *paravṛtti* from the *Lankāvatāra Sūtra,* speaks of a one hundred-eighty-degree turn-about of consciousness. Those versed in Zen celebrate the wide spaces of the new horizon it opens up to them, which surpass anything they previously knew. To the one who wrestles long with the kōan on "wu," the great nothingness opens up in a sudden breakthrough to an experience of being one with the All. The Kyoto School thinkers have sought to explicate this experience in a philosophy of emptiness. Thus Kitarō Nishida (1870–1945), inspired by Zen, made objectless pure experience the starting point of his intellectual quest, and Keiji Nishitani (1900–1990) found the ultimate ground of reality in Zen's absolute nothingness, which overcomes all forms of nihilism. Shizuteru Ueda, the chief representative of the Kyoto School today, continues to develop this original Japanese philosophy of negation, in his reflections on the break through objective being which is experienced in Zen.

At its deepest level then, the Buddhist path of knowledge becomes a negative way. The equivalent Christian negative way, rooted in silence before the ineffable and cultivated by a negative naming of God, has its ground in the Bible. Educated by the scriptural word, the Christian comes to know the transcendence of the divine being, above and beyond all finite things. This transcendence is often presented in negative terms, e.g.: "who alone has immortality and dwells in unapproachable light, whom no man has ever seen or can see" (1 Timothy 6.16); "No one has ever seen God" (John 1.18). Christian awareness of the negative force of such formulations is often dimmed by familiarity and by the poetic or metaphorical character of the language used. It is against the background of divine unknowability that the revelation of God in Jesus Christ acquires its contours: "No one knows the Son except the Father, and no one knows the Father except the Son and any one to whom the Son chooses to reveal him" (Matthew 11.27).

The Bible's constant recourse to parables and other indirect modes of communication is a practical lesson in negative theology. Is there anywhere in Scripture anything like a conceptual definition of the divine nature and the eschatological fulfilment? We constantly hear only symbolic speech. Does this not mean that the ultimate, absolute reality is best communicated in symbols, and cannot be conveyed in any other way? Hasn't Eastern religious wisdom been led by this same conviction to its particular style of negative theology? Nāgārjuna stresses the provisional character of all religious statements, and the *Lotus* and *Vimalakīrti* sūtras celebrate prowess in handling "skillful means," which can lead the mind to truth but which never capture truth in a definitive grasp. The silence of the Buddha echoes in the silence of Vimalakīrti, as the most adequate language for the knowledge of the ultimate. Zen Buddhism, drawing on all these sources, channels their apophatic wisdom into practical spiritual guidance.

The negative way pervades the whole of Buddhism, constantly pointing, in its various forms, to the reality of transcendence. The use of negation as a cipher for the unconditioned signals that human thinking, when it seeks to get a purchase on the absolute, again and again comes up against a limit. Perhaps that is why all the great religions of humanity leave a place for faith. When we realize the limits of our cognitive powers faced with the ultimate questions, then we are ready to fall back on a path of believing trust.

Shin'ichi Hisamatsu (1889–1980), one of the leading figures of the Kyoto School, who combined the theoretical knowledge of a professor of philosophy with the first-hand experience of years of meditating and teaching as a Zen master, comes, at the end of an account of the Zen way, face to face with such questions about ultimate reality.[25] The enlightened person through contemplating his own nature attains the untrammeled freedom of Zen Buddhist nothingness, no longer clinging to anything. Yet this absolutely free subject still has only limited creative power. He can create nothing original, since he does not possess the absolute creative power of God. Hisamatsu invokes the Christian doctrine, according to which God alone is the uncreated maker of all things. Only in such a being, he states, can the creative power be seen as original and absolute, yet God's existence cannot be proved; the perfect creator is an ideal or an idealization, a hypothesis or a belief. For the Christian, too, God's creative act, like his nature, is an unfathomable mystery. Christian theologians avoid anthropomorphic statements, for God does not create as an architect or an artist. Nor can philosophical arguments resolve the aporias of the idea of creation. The solution lies in faith, for which the negative way is a preparation. Convinced of the incomprehensibility of the highest being, the human heart and mind are opened for the faith that is here required.

The Essence of Buddhahood

We have seen how veneration of the Buddha, exalted to suprahuman status, opens onto the realm of transcendence. A philosophical interpretation of this religious practice was worked out by the Lokattaravādins, a group belonging to the progressive school of the Mahāsaṃghikas, who brought about the transition to Mahāyāna. The Lokattaravādins saw in Śākyamuni an earthly appearance of the supraworldly (Sanskrit: *lokattara*) Buddha. The Pali Canon itself provided some basis for such a view of Buddhahood by recognizing a multiplicity of Buddhas, whose names are listed as predecessors of Śākyamuni. From these beginnings, the bold speculative vision of Mahāyāna was able to develop a rich Buddhology, through which it sought to ground the essence of Buddhahood.

The *Lotus Sūtra* impressively dramatizes the vision of the Buddha which has shaped Mahāyāna and is still alive in Asia today. Seated at the summit of the Eagle Mount, surrounded by gods, dragon kings, and demons, and by the fourfold community of monks and nuns, lay followers male and female, the Buddha, shining in unearthly radiance, announces the wondrous Lotus dharma, in which Śākyamuni—who has entered nirvāṇa but has by no means undergone extinction—awakens from trance and with a ray of light makes visible thousands of worlds with their Buddhas and bodhisattvas. The grandiose scene which opens the sutra reveals the category of Buddhahood, to which belong the countless Buddhas of past, present, and future:

For numberless kalpas in the past,
Incalculable Buddhas, since passed into extinction,
Of a hundred thousand myriads of millions of kinds,
Their number not to be reckoned—
World-Honored Ones in this manner,
By resort to various means and parables,
To the power of these and numberless other devices (upāya)
Expound the marks of the dharmas.
These World-Honored Ones,
All preaching the Dharma of One Vehicle
Convert incalculable beings
And cause them to enter the Buddha Path.
As has been, for the Buddhas of the three ages,
The manner in which they preach the Dharma,
So I, too, now
Preach a Dharma without distinctions.[26]

While Buddhas only infrequently appear in the universe, as there can only be one Buddha in a particular world at a given time, their immeasurable number extends over infinite spaces and times, each Buddha being assigned one of the innumerable places and times. The sūtra opens up the spectacle of countless Buddha-worlds in which Buddhas, all possessing the same Buddha-essence, preach the same dharma.

In the climactic sixteenth chapter the Buddha reveals his original essence. Solemnly he declares to the assembly of great ones that those who teach that Śākyamuni left his family palace at a certain time and attained enlightenment at a certain place are not communicating the highest truth. In reality, the great enlightenment was granted him an inconceivably, immeasurably long time before. The title of this chapter is "The Lifespan of the Tathāgata": that span extends through countless world-ages into the past, and for the future the Buddha promises his helping presence, which will never expire:

> Since I attained Buddhahood,
> Throughout the number of kalpas that have passed,
> Incalculable hundred thousands of myriads
> Of million times asamkhyeyas,
> Ever have I been preaching Dharma, teaching and converting.
> Countless millions of living beings
> Have I caused to enter into the Buddha Path,
> Since which time it has been incalculable kalpas.
> For the beings' sake,
> And as an expedient device, I make a show of nirvāṇa;
> Yet in fact I do not pass into extinction,
> But ever dwell here and preach Dharma.[27]

The entry of the Buddha into nirvāṇa, these verses say, is a skillful means for rescuing those sentient beings who venerate his relics and wish to see him. The concluding parable justifies this apparent deception:

> As a physician skilled in expedient devices,
> In order to heal a son gone mad,
> Is in fact living but says he is dead,

Yet none can say he tells a willful lie,
So I, too, Father of the World that I am,
Savior from woe and suffering,
Because ordinary fellows are set on their heads,
Though I really live, say I am in extinction.[28]

The Buddha is not tied to one place, but present to many places. In other Mahāyāna writings there is much talk of Buddha lands or Buddha fields, especially those of the four directions, east, west, north, and south, that of the west, Amitābha's Pure Land, being most popular; of earlier date but lesser intensity was the devotion to Akṣobhya (Imperturbable), the Buddha of the eastern land Abhirati; the Buddhas of the northern and southern lands are also named: Amoghasiddhi (Infallible Success) and Ratnasambhava (Jewel-born). A special place is held by the Buddha Mahāvairocana, who is seen as the central Buddha of the universe in the Hua-yen school, and enjoys a similar status in Tantric Buddhism. Popular in Japanese folk piety is the healing Buddha Bhaiṣajya-guru (Yakushi).

Buddhology reaches its zenith in the *Lotus Sūtra*'s presentation of a figure pervading all times and spaces. Not only is the historical Buddha elevated to suprahuman status, but through his Buddhahood he surpasses all measure. This Buddha radiates warmth, and those who revere him and yield themselves trustingly to him are children of the Buddha, enjoying a closeness suggested by the parables of the father and the physician in the third and sixteenth chapters. The sūtra contains no philosophical statements, but the Buddha figure it presents demands to be seen in light of the doctrines of cosmic Buddha body (dharmakāya) and Buddha nature, discussed above. Transcendence and absoluteness, which are Western concepts, are not thematized in Buddhism, but their equivalents are found in many contexts. The *Lotus Sūtra,* in its overwhelming imagery, points firmly to the realm of the eternal, and holds its place in world literature along other more conceptual discourses on the transcendent.

VII

The Mystery of Personhood in Buddhist Art

We have seen that the doctrine of "non-self" has not prevented Buddhists from speaking of the true self, or of a Great Self which has a cosmic dimension and functions in synergy with the negation of the empirical self. Westerners discovered these two Asian attitudes to the self, cosmic and negative, at the same time that they were turning away from an overemphasis on historical research toward a more interior search for the spirit of India and East Asia. They cherished the hope that an assimilation of Asian values would lead to an enrichment of Western culture itself, and that the intuitive and cosmic aspects of Asian wisdom would correct the rationalist and dichotomized Western mentality. Today, only the very naive continue to hold forth on the cosmic, apersonal East, over against the man-centered, personalist West, but it does remain true that the East has an affinity for cosmic and negative expressions. However, just as one would not deny Western people all cosmic feeling for nature or acquaintance with the negative way of approaching the real, so it cannot be maintained that the person and the personal are utterly alien to Eastern thinking, especially to Buddhism.

Buddhism has always been sceptical of philosophical concepts. The Buddha had one overriding concern: to show the path of deliverance to all living beings, whom he saw ensnared in the net of suffering. Abstract discussions of personhood were irrelevant to this concern, and positively distracting. Though early Buddhist scholasticism became involved in heated discussions of the concept of person (Sanskrit: *pudgala*), this had little influence on the the mainstream of the Buddhist religion. The result is that today the speculations of Western philosophers on personhood seem remote to Eastern thinkers. It is only in the last century that Buddhist thinkers, especially in Japan, have begun to integrate these European discussions into their own speculations.

Keiji Nishitani declared that: "The idea of man as person is without doubt the highest conception of man yet to appear. The same may be said of the idea of God as person." But he went on to ask:

> Is the way of thinking about person that has so far prevailed really the only possible way of thinking about person? Put simply, until now the person has been viewed from the standpoint of the person itself. It has been a person-centered view of person [based on] a confinement of self-being to the perspective of self-immanence. . . . Person is rather a phenomenon that appears out of what cannot itself be called personal and does not entail any confinement of self-being.[1]

Nishitani calls for an "existential conversion" away from the person-centered mode of grasping person. In this letting go, "the self does not cease being a personal being." To the contrary,

> In that very conversion the personal mode of being becomes more real, draws closer to the self, and appears in its true suchness. When person-centered self-prehension is broken down and nothingness is really actualized in the self, personal existence also comes really and truly to actualization in the self. . . . Person is

> constituted at one with absolute nothingness as that in which absolute nothingness becomes manifest.[2]

Human reality can be described either in personal or impersonal terms, depending on one's perspective. Both are imperfect modes of expression, which fail us in the face of the ultimate, ineffable reality.

We shall not enter here into discussion of the philosophical questions about personhood, which in the East as in the West are beset with considerable difficulties. Instead, we shall approach some aspects of the problem of the person in Buddhism from the perspective of Buddhist art. This art and its religious significance belie the common misunderstanding of Buddhism as a completely impersonal religion.

Buddha Symbols and Buddha Images

The personalist dimension of Buddhist religiosity is clearly manifested in Buddhist art, which reveals itself as great religious art by its remarkable closeness to the living practice of piety.[3] At the center of this art is the image of the Buddha. Artistic representations of the Buddha are of two kinds: symbols such as the wheel or the stūpa, and images of his human features. Both types of representation point to the person of the Buddha and also to the ineffable meaning he embodies. As philosophical reflection was brought to bear on the personalizing representations of the Buddha, they were reabsorbed into the impersonal. In both the art and the religious thought of Buddhism, a play back and forth between personal and impersonal perspectives may be observed.

The exaltation of holy men, founders of new religions, and mighty wonder-workers into a suprahuman realm is a universal phenomenon in the history of religions. It is due to the deep human need for something constant, eternal, infinite, for spotless beauty and untroubled bliss, just the things that are sought in vain on earth. The apotheosis of Śākyamuni began soon after his entry into nirvāṇa, and is attested in stele inscriptions from the time of King Aśoka (ruled 274–236 BCE), and in the impressive artworks in Sāncī and Bhārhut (second century BCE).

Sāñcī, left by its discoverers in its natural environment, may well be the most impressive artistic site of early Buddhism. Bhārhut's treasures fill several halls of the Calcutta museum. In this most ancient form of Buddhist art, the Buddha is presented in symbolic form:

> The Buddha at birth is represented by a full blooming lotus; the Buddha in Enlightenment by the bodhi tree with a rail around it; the Buddha in his first preaching by a wheel . . . ; the Buddha in his begging round, or mendicancy, by a bowl; and the like. If suggestion be a means of true art, the early Buddhist artists understood it perfectly.[4]

Representations of the animals who marked his life's course—horse and deer, elephant and lion—reinforce the symbolic statements of this art. These symbolic evocations of the events of the Buddha's life, engraved on the gate arches, pillars, and steles in Sāñchī, vividly recalled these events to the minds of the believers. It is clear that these works rendered the Buddha himself present, especially the images of his footprints and of the Buddhist symbol par excellence, the stūpa which conceals his relics (Sanskrit: *śarīra*).[5] Hence their power to evoke responses of cultic or personal veneration, which is confirmed by the representations of worshipers, whose gestures of devotion show that the Buddha is more to them than a wise teacher; they look to him as to a suprahuman being. Such attitudes of personalized veneration are regularly observed in mainstream Buddhist tradition. The clearest testimony in ancient art is the Amaravātī sculptures of the faithful venerating the footprints of the Buddha in deep prostration. Symbols which evoke such attitudes do not originate in a completely impersonal realm, but rather testify to a suprapersonal, transcendent reality, which meets the worshiper in the symbol, claiming a veneration that involves the depth of the person.

In subsequent periods of Buddhist history these personal elements appear even more distinctly. Possibly influenced by developments in Indian religion and art outside the Buddhist tradition, Buddhists felt impelled to look for a more concrete apprehension of the object of their faith and devotion; I do not say a clearer understanding, for the abstract symbols just mentioned conveyed their meaning clearly. Representations of the Buddha in his human features fulfilled this desire for concretization. The first such images are found in the schools of Mathurā and Gandhāra; the remarkable fact that such images appeared almost simultaneously at two different places indicates that both internal and external conditions were ripe. The spread of the new iconology was rapid, and today there is not a single Asian country in which researchers and tourists do not encounter images of the Buddha. Styles developed in accord with country and historical period, yet the basic features of the image, as a visualization of great wisdom and great compassion, did not change; on this point religious practice and artistic representation dovetail.

The religious message of the image of the exalted Buddha is a compelling one. Each form of this image consolidates one of the dimensions of the religion's development. The harmonious beauty of the Gandhāra Buddha, inspired by the Hellenic spirit, is a manifestation of perfection; the dimensions of the colossal statues in Bamiyan (Afghanistan), Yüng-kang and Lungmen (China), and Nara (Japan) declare suprahuman power; the smile of Amida Buddha is an eloquent sign of compassion; the image of Śākyamuni, serenely radiant, signals enlightenment. Particularly striking are representations of a great number of Buddhas in one place (found in the Lahore and Calcutta museums), a phenomenon related to the miracle of Śrāvastī, which is recounted in the Pali Canon and often depicted in early Buddhist art. The purpose of these representations is to arouse an awareness of the suprasensible miraculous powers of the Exalted One. In the case of the fifty-six powerful Buddha heads on the towers of the massive ruins of the Bayon temple in Angkor Thom in Cambodia which look down upon the pilgrims and make them feel the presence of the Buddha as Lokeśvara, the Lord of the World, the assembly of such a great number conveys a sense of abundant personality and makes visible and palpable the Lordship and Omnipresence of the Buddha.

The Buddha image, developed in Mahāyāna into a pantheon of Buddhas and bodhisattvas, had a normative role in the formation of Buddhist folk religiosity. Through such an image, the pious were transported out of the sorrows of the impermanent world into a higher sphere. Situated in the transcendent realm and made the object of a devotion concretized in art as well as in ritual, the Buddha is the center of this piety, which took manifold forms as it spread to many countries over the centuries. An image of Buddha is the principal cult object in almost all temples of the different schools, revered with deep bowing and prostrations. In a Zen convent the nuns begin the day with a devotion in which they throw themselves down one hundred eight times before the Buddha, touching the ground with forehead, hands, and knees, showing their entire submission to the transcendent reality symbolized in his image. In accounts of Japanese Zen disciples, spontaneous expressions of reverence for the Buddha often occur. The simplest believers easily grasp the sense of the transcendence presented to them as the goal of Zen practice, and intellectuals also bow and burn incense before the image of the Buddha. As they progress in their religion they come to master also the theoretical explanation on which cult and devotion are based. Where popular religiosity necessarily concretizes the goal of religious striving, a more philosophical reflection cuts off extraneous outgrowths and reinforces the essential attitudes. Buddhism has constantly applied such reflection to popular religion, without diminishing the primordial human longing for the transcendent.

Can we say that a higher, more personalist religious life is expressed in images of the Buddha's human form? I do not think that we can answer this question with a simple yes, for the issue is many-faceted. I content myself with referring to two aspects of the matter, which are intimately connected. In the first place, the image of the Buddha does not represent the historical person, Śākyamuni, but his Buddhahood. In Theravāda this is specified by the clear marks of suprahuman greatness, while in Mahāyāna the image, in perfect accord with the Mahāyāna religious vision, is an embodiment of ultimate truth and universal salvation. In both cases the artists have correctly grasped and faithfully executed the wishes of the believers.

In the second place, even the personal image of the Buddha is in the final analysis a symbol. "While the Greeks in representing their divinities tried to bring to perfection the anthropomorphic ideal, the Indians in representing the Buddha conceived purely intellectual creations. . . . The head, for example, takes the form of the perfect oval of the egg; the eyebrows, that of the curve of an Indian bow; the eyes, that of the lotus bud; the ear, that of the graphic form of a certain Sanskrit character."[6] Easier to apprehend and more concrete than the aniconic symbols, these Buddha images still point, in virtue of their conventional stylization, to an unfathomable reality, of which they become the transparent ciphers. The most perfect realization of the Buddha type is the Buddha sitting cross-legged with hands joined in the meditation mudrā. The Buddha in the meditation posture gains "in a high degree the character and functioning of a symbol, personal now in its form."[7] The expression "personal in its form," sounds like a paradox, but leads to a deeper understanding of the relationships which obtain between symbol and person, religious practice and ultimate reality.

Person and symbol, even aniconic symbol, are not opposites. They stand to one another in a dialectical relationship, without contradicting one another. In fact, we find that in all the great religions personalistic attitudes and relationships are paralleled over long stretches of time by symbolic expressions. The preferred modes of expression depend upon the level of awareness of the believers, whether they will feel moved by their faith and piety to see the person in the symbol and to offer that person their worship, or whether, perceiving the symbolic character even of the person, especially when represented in an image, they will venerate in silence the ineffable, without reference to any object at all.

A sense of the insufficiency of the presentation can be felt to pervade artistic depictions of the Buddha, whether in abstract symbols or in his personal features. This insufficiency is thrown into high relief in the case of the symbols, which are clearly as disproportionate to what they indicate as the finger is to the moon. For the worshiper, the reality to which the symbols point remains as distant as the moon itself is from the monkey who, in the famous Zen painting, grasps at the moon reflected in the water. Despite the great skill in portrait art long developed in Europe, Westerners too have always known that all images fall short before the mystery of the person. The biblical ban on images of God reflects a similar awareness that no image can do justice to the mystery of divine personhood. At best an image is merely a "bodily prop."[8]

In comparison with other forms of Buddha worship, the personal dimension of images of Amida Buddha has a very special resonance. The raigō images elicit responses of confidence and loving abandonment. Here Amida, accompanied in the halo of his Buddha splendor by heavenly retainers, graciously comes to meet his believer from whose dying lips the nembutsu rises, in order to take him home to the Pure Land. This image, too, is of suprahuman dimensions, but, by his immeasurable mercy, the ineffably exalted Buddha inspires in his disciple confidence and joy in the process of being reborn in the Western Paradise. In these raigō images it is most frequently a monk who awaits the coming of Amida: Japanese prefer to think here of the Pure Land founder Hōnen, whom the renowned historian of religion and art, Masaharu Anesaki (1873–1949), compared with Francis of Assisi. Clearly, a deeply personal bond between worshiper and object of worship is depicted in such art.

Symbolic Hand Gestures

The image of the Buddha can be interpreted as a symbol which points in the direction of the personal without falling into anthropomorphism. This impression is strengthened by the symbols connected with the Buddha image, especially the mudrā—the hand gestures or finger positions. Historians of art find in these gestures two universes of meaning.

On the one hand, as a "seal" (the first meaning of the Sanskrit word and the one which is predominant in Esoteric thought) the mudrā proves the authenticity of the image, and its efficacy, a power which radiates from the image especially when these gestures are repeated many thousands of times by initiated officiants in a ritual cult.

But the general iconographic significance of the mudrā is more far-reaching, for it functions as a symbolic sign for doctrinal content or events, or for the totality of some Buddha figure under some particular aspect. In the context of the Buddha image, symbolic hand positions—which "derive from natural gestures made under certain conditions, such as calming by raising the hand, offering a gift be extending the arm, and so on"[9]—take on sacred meaning and religious weight. When one is able to read these signs, they function as a writing system, conveying religious attitudes more eloquently than letters can.

That the human hand has a peculiar personal expressiveness has been convincingly demonstrated by artists, thinkers, psychologists, and educators. Second only to facial features in expressive capacity, it is the most individually stamped member of the human body. Very naturally, when thoughts or emotions have to be expressed in a suitable way, the hand comes to the assistance of the word. Therefore it is safe to assume that the pious Buddhist, when he bows in worship before the image of the Buddha, senses the Exalted One speaking to him by his hand gestures and finger positions.

In Buddhism the mudrā originated as an iconographic symbol together with the Buddha images. Many mudrās indicate events of the life of the Buddha and, by the mere fact of this relation to the historical Buddha, already contain a personal element, though not always a pronounced one. The personal accent is stronger when the Buddha indicates by his gestures that he teaches his worshipers, protects them, or fulfills their wishes. Among the types of mudrā depicted in the first Buddha images in Mathurā and Gandhāra are gestures corresponding to these activities: two mudrās of gracious bestowing: the mudrā of granting wishes (lowered open left hand) and of protection (raised open right hand), and two of teaching, the mudrā of preaching (raised left hand, with thumb touching index finger; unraised cupped right hand) and of turning the wheel of doctrine (thumb touching index finger in both hands). The mudrās of gracious bestowing show the Buddha as granting the hearing of prayers and wishes, fearlessness, safety, and deliverance from anxiety. The other two also show the Buddha as one who gives something, in this case the teaching. Thus it is not surprising that the earliest Buddha images at Gandhāra do not mark sharp distinctions between the meanings of these gestures.

Later, as the mudrā spread through the Buddhist world, numerous permutations and variations developed. The mudrā of granting wishes easily combined with that of protection, especially in Chinese and Japanese statues, and the mudrā of protection was used as an expression of teaching. An important mudrā, probably invented in China, is the "mudrā that tranquilizes and gathers in (sentient beings),"[10] which is based on the preaching mudrā interpreted as a gesture of pacification. Remarkable for the fullness of its human expression, this mudrā is found in raigō images: Amida Buddha, coming to meet the believers, welcomes them to paradise and bestows his gifts upon on them with this eloquent hand gesture. The two gestures of gracious bestowing are particularly associated with Kannon, who is called the Bodhisattva of Fulfilling Wishes and Protection. Sometimes the raised right hand of the gesture of protection holds the rosary or lotus which are Kannon's attributes. The two teaching gestures pertain in the first place of course to Śākyamuni, especially the mudrā of setting in motion the wheel of the doctrine.

There are other mudrās which are strongly expressive but less strongly marked by a personal orientation toward the worshiper or contemplator: the mudrā of meditation, of the fist of knowledge, and of touching the earth in witness. If images of the Buddha can be regarded as a point of contact for the personal in Buddhism, the mudrā, especially in its communicative forms, powerfully strengthens this personalistic impact. In virtue of their "speaking function" the mudrās can be fittingly ranged with the sutras, for through them the Buddha speaks to the listening worshiper. Buddhists have always attached great importance to the hearing of this Buddha speech.

Portrait Art and Calligraphy in Zen Buddhism

In speaking of approaches to the personal in art and religious praxis, our attention has been drawn first to those approaches that directly relate to the Buddha. However, there are in Buddhism other expressions of the personal dimension, expressions that remain within the human interpersonal sphere. These too afford insights into the Buddhist sense of personhood.

Zen Buddhist portrait painting originated and developed in China as a continuation of a very ancient tradition. The oldest preserved Chinese portrait goes back to the pre-Christian era. Before and during the T'ang dynasty, a good portrait was expected to show a likeness to the original and to bring out his characteristic individuality. Though portraits of the founders and other prominent monks exist also in other Buddhist schools, Zen Buddhist portraiture is pre-eminent in the field of East Asian portrait art. Its first golden age occurs during the Southern Sung dynasty (1126–1279) and the Yüan dynasty (1280–1368). In Japan its golden age began in the Kamakura period and reached its apogee during the Muromachi period (1336–1573). Particularly at times of high creativity the Zen painters endeavored in their portraits to represent and bring to life the revered patriarchs and masters with their personal idiosyncrasies. In his very instructive and penetrating study of Zen Buddhist portraiture in China and Japan, Helmut Brinker declares that "in the broad field of Zen the historical personality and the person in general stepped into the center of thought and conduct."[11]

The Zen portrait draws its aesthetic force from several roots. First, there is the distinct consciousness of tradition whereby the spirit of this school is transmitted from generation to generation in an uninterrupted chain from Śākyamuni to his disciple Kāśyapa, first of the twenty-eight

Indian patriarchs, and from the last of these, Bodhidharma, to his Chinese and Japanese successors. The first six Chinese patriarchs are frequently portrayed in the "generation paintings," a cycle which was a favorite theme. The cycle is extended beyond Lin-chi all the way to the contemporary abbots and Zen masters of Chinese and Japanese monasteries. In these works the traditional lineage is the focus of interest, and the individual recedes for the simple reason that these are almost purely ideal pictures, often based on legendary traits of their subjects.

The transmission of the Zen spirit also plays another role in the motivation of portrait painting. It had become customary quite early, upon a disciple's attainment of enlightenment, for the master to present the disciple with a picture of himself, preferably adorned with an autographic inscription. This portrait was intended to keep alive the memory of the strict guidance of the master and of the great moment of enlightenment, thus spurring the disciple on to ever deeper insights on the path of spiritual discipline. The portrait also came to be considered as a certificate of the authenticity of the disciple's enlightenment experience. It was because there was a danger of deviating from the unconventional spiritual way of Zen that such eminent masters as Dōgen and Ikkyū strenuously objected against the abuse of these certificates of enlightenment (though Ikkyū himself probably gave away some portaits as certificates). I prefer to see these portraits—whatever the inscriptions declare—as witnesses to the cordial relationship between master and disciple in Zen. Dietrich Seckel, an eminent art historian, draws our attention insistently to this personal dimension:

> The portraiture of arhats, patriarchs, and priests was promoted with great vigor by adherents of the Ch'an school, which attached great importance to deeply religious personages, to the contact between master and pupils, and to the handing on of traditions "from mind to mind." In this case the chain of tradition plays an enhanced role and is based entirely on personal relationships.[12]

Finally, Zen portraits, especially those of patriarchs and founding abbots, are used in the temple-monasteries as pictures before which ritual acts are performed. Hence, they resemble the paintings of early Buddhist saints or arhats, to which they are also related in artistic style.[13] They often occupy a place of honor in a niche of a main temple hall, and sometimes they even have their own separate building among the numerous buildings scattered over the temple grounds, which serve partly a cultic and partly a practical purpose. When thus enshrined in a "dim religious light" these works of art are not readily accessible to the connoisseur. This may have something to do with the fact that Zen portrait art became known late, actually only in the last decades, although what are termed "priest portraits"—mostly full-length pictures of founders, abbots, and masters in priestly attire—had always enjoyed great popularity in the Japanese Zen monasteries.

In many of its best works this tradition of portraiture allows the viewer to meet a real person. According to the kind of portrait, the individuality of the subjects emerges more or less strongly and in different ways. One does not have to be an expert to be impressed by the characteristic vitality of expression of these portraits. Even in the posthumous, ideal portraits of the patriarchs one is surprised at the liveliness and differentiation of the faces. Brinker admires one "lovable, youthfully fresh, and appealing face with an expression of understanding mildness and wisdom," and notes that in a transfiguration picture, the facial features of Zen master Daichi Kojin (1290–1366), figuring here as Bodhisattva Kṣitigarbha (Jizō), are "entirely individual and not formed after the idealized schema of the Jizō figure."[14]

The specific portrait typology in Zen painting did not impede the elaboration of individual, characteristic features, for Zen painters were concerned with seizing the true individual being of their subjects. This is especially true of the portraits of Zen masters painted by their talented disciples. From the wealth of individual portraits executed during the lifetime of the master portrayed, I shall select the portraits of three personalities who were prominent in the history of Zen Buddhism. Two original portraits of the famous Chinese Zen master, Hsü-t'ang Chih-yü (1185–1269)—painted by unknown Chinese artists who must have been personally acquainted with the master and adorned with an inscription by the master himself—were given by the master to Japanese disciples, who brought them to Japan, where they are now to be found in the famous Zen monasteries of Myōshinji and Daitokuji in Kyoto. According to Brinker, the Myōshinji portrait, dated 1258, communicates "in an outstanding way an impression of the looks of this serious, good-natured, and tolerant Ch'an master."[15] The Daitokuji portrait, picturing the master as an octogenarian, is scarcely less praiseworthy. It appears to be better preserved and shows the facial features in sharper outline.

Musō Soseki (1275–1351), better known by the honorary title, Musō Kokushi (national master Musō), conferred on him by the Emperor Go-Daigo, is the dominating figure in Japanese Zen during the first half of the fourteenth century. His powerful initiative assured that the Zen tradition, imported from China, would become a constitutive element in Japanese culture.

> Once in a thousand years
> the Udambara blooms
> It has opened its auspicious flowers
> Many labored
> to bring it
> from India to Japan
> Its heady fragrance
> lingers
> without fading
> and is not lost
> amid the thousand grasses
> the countless weeds[16]

Soseki is without equal in the combination, so typical of Zen, of spirituality, culture, and artistic talent. Many portraits of him attest to the veneration and affection his contemporaries felt for him. In these works the spiritualized, ascetic features bespeak the inner-directed insight of this enlightened monk. The aristocratic distinction of his upright posture makes his influence as educator and popular leader understandable. The fact that this leading personality was himself a creative artist of the first rank spurred his portraitists to give of their best and to be as faithful as possible to the model. The gaunt, wrinkled face of the bald-headed master in the portrait of the sixty-five-year-old Soseki at Tenryūji is alive through the clear, kindly, quiet gaze of the eyes. His disciple Mutō Shūi (fl. 1346–69) painted the most famous portrait of Soseki, bringing out the open spiritual attitude of the master in the gravity of his countenance. Musō Kokushi's name is linked with a number of famous monasteries, and traces of his artistic activity can be found in places all over Japan.

The most popular of all Japanese Zen masters, Ikkyū Sōjun, inspired the greatest number of portraits, exhibiting the broadest spectrum of iconographic types and styles of expression. Some twenty have been preserved, and they show the master in a variety of guises. Given his eccentric character, it is not surprising that they are marked by a high degree of individuality. In the early works, he is shown with a fully shaved head as the strict monastic rule prescribes, but even here he squats indolently with legs half crossed, while a long wooden sword, added as his distinguishing emblem, symbolizes, according to his own explanation, the hypocrisy of contemporary Zen, which lacks the quality of a real sword. Later generations have been most impressed by a portrait sketch ascribed to his trusted disciple Bokusai (1412–92). In this half-length portrait, the master, with head turned to the left, watches the viewer from the corner of his eyes, "the look is penetrating rather than dignified,"[17] the hair stands up, and under the big nose with the extraordinary large nostrils a hairy beard and mustache protrude. There have been other long-haired Zen masters, and Ikkyū continues on this point the line of the founder of this school, Lin-chi. In another portrait, thought to be by Bokusai and kept in the Shuon'an, the features are exquisitely drawn and betray something of Ikkyū's spirited and pointed humor; dating from the time he was called to be abbot of Daitokuji, it served as a model for other similar works. Another work of the same period shows the master, who was the enemy of all convention and whose style of life was in mocking contrast to the pomp and corruption he saw in his contemporaries, in formal priestly attire. Brinker comments on this work:

> With a penetrating, critically probing, altogether challenging glare, the man in the portrait looks at the viewer from the corner of his eyes. For Zen portraits this is a highly unusual trait, which nonetheless intensifies to a high degree of liveliness the direct communication between the viewed and the viewer.[18]

Zen painting underwent a revival about the middle of the Edo period, but the forte of the two greatest figures here, Hakuin (1685–1768) and Sengai (1750–1837), did not lie in portraiture. Sengai's Chinese-style ink paintings (*sumie*) depict realistic and humorous episodes, caricatures of people in comic situations, uncommon natural phenomena. He illustrated in a tasteful way many Zen verses, utterances of the masters, and kōan. Hakuin's religious fame has overshadowed his greatness as a master of sumie and calligraphy. There are also a number of valuable portraits from his brush. In this autumn of Zen portraiture the perfection of the Muromachi period could no longer be attained; nevertheless Hakuin's self-portraits remain astounding: the enormous penetrating eyes with which the master, warning stick in hand, stares straight ahead of him or into the distance, impress themselves unforgettably. Hardly ever has the spiritual force which flows from meditation and kōan practice been represented in a more striking way. If it be true that "every self-portrait proceeds from and points back to a self-aware individual," then the self-portraits which are current in Zen attest that "man has become fully conscious of his own person and personality."[19]

Zen personality is expressed not only in images but in the spoken and written word. Shaped as we are by the logos, Western people cherish the conviction that nothing reveals the person in its essence like the word and language. In this perspective, it would be worthwhile to consider the linguistic achievements within Buddhism—beginning with the sutras and śāstras, moving to the written testimonies of later generations, and finishing with the forceful utterances of the Zen masters. In

East Asian Buddhism, the word has a bearing on the personal similar to that of the image, for word and image are closely linked. The East Asian sees in the written character a word penetrating to the deepest essence of things. When a Zen master wants to share the most precious treasure of his wisdom and to give his disciple a special token of his friendship, he will squat for a moment in the meditation posture and then—with the greatest concentration, often in a few swift strokes of compressed force—write a character and hand the written paper to his friend.

> The Zen characters—normal Chinese characters freely selected and reshaped in an original way—in their vital and often dynamic application of the brush stroke, do not only give direct expression to the personality of the writer, but equally show the degree of his insight and spiritual power.[20]

For this reason, calligraphy (*shodō,* the way of writing), a craft brought to perfection in East Asian Buddhism, must be reckoned among the artistic aspects of the problem of the person in Buddhism.

The Access to the Person Through Art

The individuality and personality of the represented subject in portraiture seems to depend on the skill of the artist, as can be deduced from the vividness of the pictures of arhats and long-dead patriarchs. Often such portraits leave much food for thought, as neither the intention of the artist nor the ultimate symbolic upshot of the work are easily deciphered. Zen art testifies to a keen sense of the mystery of personhood, though it reached its highest peaks in landscape painting, suggesting that the cosmic sense of nature enjoyed priority.

Within Buddhism there is ample space for a humane ethics which values human rights and nurtures compassionate concern for human advancement. The objection is often made against Buddhist humanism that in its presentation of the cycle of incarnations, which includes animals, hungry ghosts, hells, and other states of being, the special position of human beings in the universe is not taken into account and does not carry much weight. Yet among modern Buddhists, who treat much of this lore as mythological, the privileged position of humans among all living beings is at the center of ethical consciousness. The word *jinkaku,* meaning "person," occurs frequently in Japanese sermons and instructions.

Far more difficult is the question concerning the personal or impersonal character of ultimate reality. Although mainstream Buddhism recognizes a transcendent, absolute reality, there is a reluctance to ascribe a personal character to it. In the Buddhist way of thinking, the personal attitudes in Buddhist religious praxis are not sufficient to justify the recognition of a personal Supreme Being. On this point, the dialogue between Buddhists and Christians is not very promising. Even after removal of the anthropomorphic character of the idea of a personal God and the limitations of the philosophical concept of person, Buddhists remain unpersuaded that the ineffable ultimate—whether one calls it nirvāṇa, Buddha nature, emptiness, or nothingness—can ever be compatible with the associations of the word "person." This is true for all forms of Buddhism, Amida Buddhism not excluded.

Whether, in its deepest ground, being is personal or impersonal, is something that humans will never be able to plumb by their rational powers. Here we face a decision which one makes according to one's tradition and upbringing, and still more according to one's faith and experience. The Christian sees ultimate reality revealed in the personal love of God as shown in Christ, the Buddhist in the silence of the Buddha. Yet they agree on two things: that the ultimate mystery is ineffable, and that it should be manifest to human beings. The inscription on a Chinese stone figure of the Buddha, dated 746, reads:

> The highest truth is without image.
> If there were no image at all, however, there would be no way for truth to be manifested.
> The highest principle is without words.
> But if there were not words at all, how could principle possibly be revealed?[21]

Notes

Chapter 1

1. Heinrich Dumoulin, *Zen Buddhism: A History,* 2 vols. (New York: Macmillan, 1988, 1990). I have been working recently on an expanded version of the first volume, and some of the new material has appeared in *Japanese Journal of Religious Studies* 20:1 (1993). See also *Zen Buddhism in the 20th Century* (New York and Tokyo: Weatherhill, 1992).

2. The present work is largely based on the previously untranslated sections of *Begegnung mit dem Buddhismus,* second edition (Freiburg: Herder, 1991), and it can be seen as a supplement or sequel to *Encounter with Buddhism* (Lasalle: Open Court, 1974, reprinted 1990).

3. Robert A. F. Thurman, *The Central Philosophy of Tibet* (Princeton, New Jersey: Princeton University Press, 1991), 19. For a sense of how offensive the term "Hīnayāna" is to Theravāda Buddhists, see David J. Kalupahana, *A History of Buddhist Philosophy* (Honolulu: University of Hawaii Press, 1992), 238–39.

4. The standard work is Alfred Foucher, *L'art gréco-bouddhique du Gandhāra,* 4 vols. (Paris: E. Leroux, 1905–1922); see also John Marshall, *The Buddhist Art of Gandhāra* (Cambridge: Cambridge University Press, 1960).

5. Émile Bréhier, *La philosophie de Plotin* (Paris: Vrin, 1961).

6. Charles Eliot, *Hinduism and Buddhism* (London: Routledge & Kegan Paul, 1921) 3:265; *Japanese Buddhism* (Routledge & Kegan Paul, 1935), 148–50, 394–95.

7. Henri de Lubac, *Amida* (Paris: Editions du Seuil, 1955), discusses these resemblances, but comes to a negative conclusion. On the general theme of this chapter see de Lubac's *La Rencontre du Bouddhisme et de l'Occident* (Paris: Aubier, 1952).

8. *Sinica Franciscana* vol. 1, ed. Anastasius van den Wyngaert (Florence: Quaracchi, 1929), 229–32.

9. See *Zen Buddhism: A History* 2:262–70.

10. S.G. Schurhammer, *Die Disputationen des P. Cosme de Torres mit den Buddhisten im Jahre 1551* (Tokyo: Deutsche Gesellschaft für Natur- und Völkerkunde Ostasiens, 1929).

11. Raimundo Panikkar, *The Intrareligious Dialogue* (New York: Paulist, 1978), xxv–xxvi.

12. *Documents of Vatican II,* ed. Austin P. Flannery (Grand Rapids: Eerdmans, 1975), 738.

13. *Der Herr* (Würzburg: Werbund, 1937), 410–11.

14. *Documents of Vatican II,* 738–9.

Chapter 2

1. Heinz Bechert, "The Date of the Buddha Reconsidered," *Indologica Taurinensia* 10 (1982), 29–36. For the formation of the Buddha's biography, see Edward J. Thomas, *The Life of Buddha in Legend and History* (London: Routledge & Kegan Paul, 1975); Étienne Lamotte, *History of Indian Buddhism* (Louvain-la-Neuve: Institut Orientaliste, 1988), 639–85.

2. See *The Middle Length Sayings,* trans. I.B. Horner (London: Pali Text Society, 1954), 1: 207.

3. *The Sutta-Nipāta,* trans. H. Saddhatissa (London: Curzon Press, 1985), 48–49.

4. Quoted in Thomas, *The Life of Buddha,* 67–68. See *Middle Length Sayings* 1:303.

5. *Middle Length Sayings* 1:216.

6. *Buddhist* Scriptures, trans. Edward Conze (Harmondsworth: Penguin, 1976), 186.

7. *Die buddhistische Versenkung* (Munich, 1922), 16.

8. Takeuchi, *The Heart of Buddhism,* trans. James Heisig (New York: Crossroad, 1983), 19.

9. Ibid., 20.

10. For a translation of the twelvefold chain into concrete psychological terms, see Rune Johansson, *The Psychology of Nirvana* (London: Allen & Unwin, 1969).

11. Hermann Oldenberg, *Buddha: His Life, His Doctrine, His Order* (New Delhi: Indological Book House, 1971), 212.

12. Quoted in Guy Richard Welbon, *The Buddhist Nirvāna and Its Western Interpreters* (Chicago: University of Chicago Press, 1968), 165. For a fresh look at Schopenhauer see my article "Buddhism and Nineteenth-Century German Philosophy," *Journal of the History of Ideas* 42 (1981), 457–70.

13. Keiji Nishitani, *Religion and Nothingness*, trans. Jan Van Bragt (Berkeley: University of California Press, 1982).

14. See, for example, Ulrich Schneider, *Einführung in den Buddhismus* (Darmstadt: Wissenschaftliche Buchgesellschaft, 1980), 72.

15. See Kalupahana, *A History of Buddhist Philosophy*, 96.

16. *Middle Length Sayings* 2:166.

17. *The Sutta-Nipāta*, 123; see Peter Harvey, *An Introduction to Buddhism* (Cambridge: Cambridge University Press, 1990), 66–67.

18. Walpola Rahula, *What the Buddha Taught* (New York: Grove Press, 1974), 51.

19. Oldenberg, *Buddha*, 211.

20. See Ernst Waldschmidt, *Von Ceylon bis Turfan* (Göttingen: Vandenhock & Ruprecht, 1967), 375–90. André Bareau, in his *Recherches sur la Biographie du Buddha* (Paris: Publications de l'École Française d'Extrême-Orient, 1963), gives a complete translation of the oldest traditions about the enlightenment of Śākyamuni, comprising one Theravāda sūtra, one Sarvastivāda sūtra, an "anonymous sūtra" and two vinaya texts. All of these explicitly speak of the Four Noble Truths as the expression of the Buddha's enlightenment, but none mentions the five skandhas (see 75–79, 392).

21. Harvey, *An Introduction to Buddhism*, 51.

22. *The Book of the Discipline* 4, trans. I.B. Horner (London: Pali Text Society, 1951), 4:21 (slightly modified).

23. *The Questions of King Milinda*, trans. T.W. Rhys Davids (Oxford: Oxford University Press, 1890), 44–45.

24. T. Stcherbatsky, *The Central Conception of Buddhism and the Meaning of the Word "Dharma"* (London: Royal Asiatic Society, 1923); O. Rosenberg, *Probleme der buddhistischen Philosophie* (Heidelberg: Harrassowitz, 1924).

25. *The Heart of Buddhism*, 20.

26. "The Basic Teachings of Buddhism," in: *Buddhism in the Modern World*, ed. H. Dumoulin and John Maraldo (New York: Macmillan, 1976), 3–31; here 9–11.

27. Joaquín Peréz-Remón, *Self and Non-Self in Early Buddhism* (The Hague: Mouton, 1980), 304.

28. E. Conze, *Buddhist Thought in India* (Ann Arbor: University of Michigan Press, 1982), 39.

29. Ibid., 122.

30. Ibid., 130.

31. See Lynn A. de Silva, *The Problem of the Self in Buddhism and Christianity* (New York: Barnes & Noble, 1979); Steven Collins, *Selfless Persons: Imagery and Thought in Theravāda Buddhism* (Cambridge: Cambridge University Press, 1982); "Self and Non-Self in Early Buddhism," *Numen* 28 (1982), 250–61.

32. See D.T. Suzuki, *Essays in Zen Buddhism* 1 (London: Rider, 1958), 241.

33. Quoted in Robert E. Buswell, *The Zen Monastic Experience* (Princeton: Princeton University Press, 1992), 154.

34. Enomiya-Lassalle, *Zen-Buddhismus* (Cologne: Bachem, 1966), 398.

35. *Confessions,* trans. Henry Chadwick (Oxford: Oxford University Press, 1991), 123.

36. Thomas Merton, *The Ascent to Truth* (New York: Harcourt Brace, 1951), 197.

37. W. Gundert, *Bi-yän-lu* (Munich: Hanser, 1960–73), 2:156, 169–70.

Chapter 3

1. E. Conze, *Buddhism: Its Essence and Development* (London: Faber and Faber, 1951), 94.

2. Quoted in Gilles Quispel, "Gnosticism," *The Encyclopedia of Religion,* ed. Mircea Eliade (New York: Macmillan, 1987), 5:566.

3. Marion L. Matics, trans., *Entering the Path of Enlightenment: The Bodhicaryāvatāra of the Buddhist Poet Sāntideva* (New York: Macmillan, 1970).

4. E. Conze et al., ed., *Buddhist Texts through the Ages,* (New York: Harper and Row, 1964), 52.

5. Ibid., 53–54.

6. Ibid., 52.

7. *Middle Length Sayings* 1:46.

8. Yoshito S. Hakeda, trans., *The Awakening of Faith in the Mahayana* (Columbia University Press, 1967), 92.

9. *The Sutta-Nipāta,* 131–32.

10. *Buddhist Texts Through the Ages,* 51–52.

11. D.T. Suzuki, *Shin Buddhism: Japan's Major Religious Contribution to the West* (New York: Harper and Row, 1970); see also his *Collected Writings on Shin Buddhism* (Kyoto: Shinshū-Ōtani, 1973), and his essays in *The Eastern Buddhist,* 1980, 1981, 1985, 1990.

12. For an annotated trilingual edition of the latter text (which is extant only in Chinese), see *The Sutra of Contemplation on the Buddha of Immeasurable Life* (Kyoto: Ryūkoku University, 1984); a translation by Junjirō Takakusu of all three sutras can be found in *Sacred Books of the East,* vol. 49.

13. See Alfred Bloom, *Shinran's Gospel of Pure Grace* (Tucson: University of Arizona Press, 1965), and Takamichi Takahatake, *Young Man Shinran* (Ontario: Wilfred Laurier University Press, 1987).

14. Dennis Hirota, trans., *Tannishō: A Primer,* (Kyoto: Ryūkoku University, 1982), 23. For the subsequent ecclesiastical development of Shinran's faith see James Carter Dobbins, *Jōdo Shinshū: Shin Buddhism in Medieval Japan* (Bloomington: Indiana University Press, 1989). The most formative agent in this development was the indefatigable Rennyo (1415–99); see Minor and Ann Rogers, *Rennyo: The Second Founder of Shin Buddhism* (Berkeley, California: Asian Humanities Press, 1991).

15. Hirota, 22.

16. Ibid., 31.

17. Yoshifumi Ueda, ed., *The True Teaching, Practice and Realization of the Way,* 2 vols. (Kyoto: Hongwanji International Center, 1983), 160–67.

18. Ibid.

19. Ibid.

20. See Bloom, 18-19.

21. Ueda, loc. cit.

22. Quoted in Bloom, 63.

23. Hirota, 37, 38.

24. For insights on the problems of a dialogue between Pure Land Buddhists and Christians, see Jan van Bragt, "Buddhism—Jōdo Shinshū—Christianity: Does Jōdo Shinshū form a bridge between Buddhism and Christianity," *Japanese Religions* 18 (1993), 47–75.

25. In recent years a notable contribution along these lines has been made by the influential writings of the Sri Lankan Jesuit Aloysius Pieris. See his *Love Meets Wisdom: A Christian Experience of Buddhism* (Maryknoll: Orbis, 1988), and *An Asian Theology of Liberation* (Maryknoll: Orbis, 1988).

Chapter 4

1. On Buddhist ethics see Shundo Tachibana, *The Ethics of Buddhism* (New York: Barnes and Noble, 1975); H. Saddhatissa, *Buddhist Ethics* (London: Allen & Unwin, 1970).

2. *Buddhist* Scriptures, trans. Conze, 51–52.

3. Ibid., 58.

4. *The Sutta-Nipāta,* 16, verses 4-5.

5. Ibid., verse 6.

6. Ibid., verse 7.

7. Ibid., verses 8–9.

8. Quoted in Paravihara Vajirañaṇa, *Buddhist Meditation* (Kuala Lumpur: Buddhist Missionary Society, 1975), 268.

9. *The Dhammapada,* trans. John Ross Carter and Mahinda Palihawadana (Oxford University Press, 1987), 35.

10. *Die buddhistische Versenkung,* 23.

11. Quoted in Richard Gombrich, *Theravāda Buddhism* (London: Routledge & Kegan Paul, 1988), 64.

12. *The Iti-vuttaka,* trans. Justin Hartley Moore (New York: AMS Press, repr. 1965).

13. *Buddhist Texts through the Ages,* 65; for several other texts on wisdom, see 51-65.

14. Conze, *Buddhism,* 129.

15. Ibid., 108–9.

16. Robert A.F. Thurman, *The Holy Teaching of Vimalakīrti* (Pennsylvania State University Press, 1976), 56–57.

17. See C.N. Tay, "Kuan-Yin: The Cult of Half Asia," *History of Religions* 16 (1976), 147–77; John C. Holt, *Buddha in the Crown: Avalokiteśvara in the Buddhist Traditions of Sri Lanka* (Oxford University Press, 1991).

18. See *Sutra of the Past Vows of Earth Store Bodhisattva* (New York: Buddhist Text Translation Society, 1974); Yoshiko Kurata Dykstra, "Jizō, the Most Merciful," *Monumenta Nipponica* 33 (1978), 179–200.

19. See Michael Pye, *Skilful Means* (London: Duckworth, 1978).

20. *Scripture of the Lotus Blossom of the Fine Dharma,* trans. Leon Hurvitz (New York: Columbia University Press, 1976), 59.

21. Ibid., 63.

22. Ibid., 74.

23. Ibid., 87.

24. Ibid., 88.

25. See Yoshito S. Hakeda, trans. *Kūkai: Major Works* (Columbia University Press, 1972), 151–57.

26. Ibid., 87.

27. Ibid., 96.

28. There is a famous story about the enlightenment of Lin-chi (d. 866), who was struck and dismissed three times by his master Huang-po. His reaction: "It was so kind of you to send me to question the master. Three times I asked him and three times I was hit by him. I regret that some obstruction caused by my own past karma prevents me from grasping his profound meaning." Eventually, in extreme misery, he underwent the liberating enlightenment. Dumoulin, *Zen Buddhism: A History* 1:182.

29. Ibid., 2:371.

30. See Bloom, 84.
31. Suzuki, *Shin Buddhism,* 77–78.
32. *Udāna* quoted in Conze, *Buddhist Thought in India,* 212.
33. *The Dhammapada,* trans. Carter and Palihawadana, 13, 51.

Chapter 5

1. Nyanoponika Thera, *The Heart of Buddhist Meditation* (London: Rider, 1975).

2. *The Path of Freedom,* trans. N.R.M. Ehara, Soma Thera, and Kheminda Thera (Colombo: Deerasuriya, 1961). This is from the sixth-century Chinese translation; the original Pali work is no longer extant.

3. *The Path of Purification,* trans. Bhikkhu Ñāṇamoli (Berkeley: Shambala, 1976).

4. Nyanaponika, *The Heart of Buddhist Meditation,* 117.

5. Ibid., 117–18.

6. Nyanatiloka, *Buddhistisches Wörterbuch* (Konstanz, 1953), 244.

7. On the meditation sūtras, see Hajime Nakamura, *Indian Buddhism: A Survey with Bibliographical Notes* (Delhi: Motilal Banarsidass, 1987), 171–74.

8. Leon Hurvitz, *Chih-i (538–597): An Introduction to the Life and Ideas of a Chinese Buddhist Monk* (Brussels: Institut Belge des Hautes Études Chinoises, 1980), 271–72.

9. Ibid., 274.

10. William R. LaFleur, *The Karma of Words* (University of California Press, 1983), 92–93.

11. Hurvitz, *Chih-i,* 272–73.

12. See Neal Donner, "Sudden and Gradual Intimately Conjoined: Chih-i's T'ien-t'ai View," in: *Sudden and Gradual Approaches to Enlightenment in Chinese Thought,* ed. Peter N. Gregory (Honolulu: University of Hawaii Press, 1987), 204.

13. Ibid., 205.

14. Quoted in Daniel B. Stevenson, "The Four Kinds of Samādhi in Early T'ien-t'ai Buddhism," in: *Traditions of Meditation in Chinese Buddhism,* ed. Peter N. Gregory (Honolulu: University of Hawaii Press, 1986), 49.

15. Quoted in Donner, "Sudden and Gradual Intimately Conjoined," 214–15.

16. Stevenson, "The Four Kinds of Samādhi," 58.

17. Ibid., 60.

18. Quoted in Donner, "Sudden and Gradual Intimately Conjoined," 216.

19. Ibid., 218.

20. Ibid., 203. For the preceding account of T'ien-t'ai meditation I am also

indebted to Shindai Sekiguchi, *Tendai Shikan no Kenkyū* (Tokyo: Iwanami Shoten, 1969). See also Neal Donner, *The Great Calming and Contemplation:* A Study & Annotated Translation of the First Chapter of Chih-i's "Mo-Lo chih-kuan" (Honolulu: University of Hawaii Press 1993), Paul L. Swanson, *Foundations of T'ien-t'ai Philosophy* (Berkeley: Asian Humanities Press, 1989).

21. A good account of Shingon is Minoru Kiyota, *Shingon Buddhism: Theory and Practice* (Los Angeles, Tokyo: Buddhist Books International, 1978).

22. Lama Anagarika Govinda, *Mandala,* 4th ed. (Bern: Origo, 1984), 26–27.

23. Hakeda, *Kūkai: Major Works,* 263.

24. Ibid., 231.

25.Nakamura, *Indian Buddhism,* 205; see also Paul Williams, *Mahāyāna Buddhism: The Doctrinal Foundations* (London and New York: Routledge, 1989), 217–21.

26. *The Sutra of Contemplation on the Buddha of Immeasurable Life,* 63.

27. Quoted in Ryosetsu Fujiwara, *The Way to Nirvana: The Concept of the Nembutsu in Shan-tao's Pure Land Buddhism* (Tokyo: Kyoiku Shinchosha, 1974), 27.

28. Ibid., 26.

29. *The Sutra of Contemplation on the Buddha of Immeasurable Life,* 109.

30. Fujiwara, *The Way to Nirvana,* 62.

31. Ibid., 104.

32. Ibid., 106.

33. Ibid., 157.

34. Quoted in Daigan and Alicia Matsunaga, *Foundations of Japanese Buddhism* (Los Angeles, Tokyo: Buddhist Books International, 1976) 2:59.

35. See Alexander El'chaninov, *The Diary of a Russian Pilgrim* (London, 1967).

36. See Carl Bielefeldt, *Dōgen's Manuals on Zen Meditation* (Berkeley, Los Angeles, London: University of California Press, 1988).

37. Author's translation. See Bielefeldt, 177.

38. See Bielefeldt, 181.

39. Trans. Masunaga Reihō, *A Primer of Sōtō Zen* (Honolulu: University of Hawaii Press, 1971), 47.

40. Quoted in Dumoulin, *Zen Buddhism: A History* 1:85.

41. See Anthony de Mello, *Sadhana: A Way to God* (New York: Doubleday, 1984).

42. Ibid., 35.

43. Ibid., 11.

44. Ibid., 46.

45. Hugh M. Enomiya-Lassalle, *Zen Meditation for Christians* (La Salle, Illinois: Open Court, 1974), 8–9. See Dumoulin, *Zen Buddhism in the 20th Century,* 103–38, for a discussion of Zen meditation in Christian perspective.

46. J.L. Kadowaki, *Zen and the Bible* (Penguin: Arkana, 1990).

Chapter 6

1. Quoted by Steven Collins, *Selfless Persons,* 130.

2. *Middle Length Sayings* 2:98–9.

3. *Bṛhad-āraṇyaka Upanishad* 3: 9, 26; 4: 2, 4; 4: 4, 22; 4: 5, 15.

4. Quoted in Raimundo Panikkar, *The Vedic Experience* (London: Darton, Longman & Todd, 1977), 87, 40.

5. *Middle Length Sayings* 2:165–66.

6. In *Buddhism in the Modern World,* 21.

7. For the most important text, with an English translation, see Kenneth K. Inada, *Nāgārjuna: A Translation of his Mūlamadhyamakakārikā* (Tokyo: Hokuseido, 1970).

8. See Williams, *Mahāyāna Buddhism,* 37–76.

9. T.R.V. Murti, *The Central Philosophy of Buddhism: A Study of the Mādhyamika System* (London: Allen & Unwin, 1955), 129.

10. Erich Frauwallner, *Die Philosophie des Buddhismus* (Berlin: Akademie-Verlag, 1969) 2:184.

11. The quotations from Candrakīrti are from *Buddhist Texts through the Ages,* 168–69.

12. As LaFleur cautions: "Once Platonism is imported into Buddhist thought as though it were a useful tool for getting a handle on things, it begins to act like a philosophical equivalent of the sorcerer's apprentice, fomenting misconceptions all over the place" (*The Karma of Words,* 89).

13. Quoted by Junjirō Takakusu, *The Essentials of Buddhist Philosophy* (University of Hawaii Press, 1956), 48.

14. *The Iti-vuttaka,* trans. Moore, 109. "That monk seeth the Law, and seeing the Law, he seeth me."

15. *Buddhist Texts through the Ages,* 144.

16. Ibid., 211.

17. Ibid., 183.

18. *Ratnagotravibhāga,* cited by Brian Edward Brown, *The Buddha Nature: A Study of the Tathāgatagarbha and Ālayavijñāna* (Delhi, 1991), 56.

19. See ibid., 107. The Sanskrit terms *gotra* and *garbha* designate the seed or the embryo; *cittaprakṛti* designates the noetic substratum.

20. Trans. Norman Waddell and Masao Abe, *The Eastern Buddhist* 4:2 (1971), 113.

21. For more on Hua-yen, see G.C.C. Chang, *The Buddhist Teaching of Totality: The Philosophy of Hwa Yen* (Pennsylvania State University Press, 1971); Francis H. Cook, *Hua-yen Buddhism: The Jewel Net of Indra* (Pennsylvania State University Press, 1977).

22. Author's translation.

23. Author's translation. See Zenkei Shibayama, *Zen Comments on the Mumonkan* (San Francisco: Harper & Row, 1974).

24. "Shōbōgenzō Buddha-nature," trans. M. Abe and N. Waddell, *The Eastern Buddhist* 9 (1976), 73, 76–77.

25. Shin'ichi Hisamatsu, *Die Fülle des Nichts* (Pfullingen: Neske, 1975).

26. *Scripture of the Lotus Blossom,* 37, 45. The reference to the essence of Buddhahood is clearer in the original Sanskrit: "As the dharmahood of those former Saviors and of the Victorious Ones to come, by me also has it [my dharmahood] been freed of discrimination, and just so have I showed it to you" (ibid. 353).

27. Ibid., 242.

28. Ibid., 244.

Chapter 7

1. Nishitani, *Religion and Nothingness,* 69.

2. Ibid., 71.

3. The remainder of this chapter reproduces material from my essay, "The Person in Buddhism: Religious and Artistic Aspects," trans. Jan Van Bragt, *Japanese Journal of Religious Studies* 11 (1984), 143–67.

4. Takakusu, *Essentials of Buddhist Philosophy,* 50.

5. For an explanation of the symbols see Dietrich Seckel, *Jenseits des Bildes: Anikonische Symbolik in der buddhistischen Kunst* (Heidelberg: Abhandlungen der Heidelberger Akademie, 1976).

6. Ibid., 14.

7. Ibid., 20.

8. One finds this expression in Tibetan Buddhism (ibid., 40).

9. E. Dale Saunders, *Mudrā: A Study of Symbolic Gestures in Japanese Buddhism* (Princeton University Press, 1960), 10.

10. See ibid., 69.

11. Helmut Brinker, *Die zen-buddhistische Bildnismalerei in China und Japan* (Wiesbaden: Franz Steiner Verlag, 1973), 18.

12. Dietrich Seckel, "Buddha-Symbole und Buddha-Kult," in *Religion und Religionen* (Festschrift Gustav Mensching, Bonn, 1967), 254.

13. See Kurt Brasch, *Zenga* (Tokyo: Japanisch–Deutsche Gesellschaft, 1961), 14–15.

14. Brinker, *Die zen-buddhistische Bildnismalerei,* 104, 87.

15. Ibid., 117.

16. Musō Soseki, *Sun at Midnight,* trans. W.S. Merwin and Soiku Shigematsu (San Francisco: North Point Press, 1989), 101.

17. Donald Keene, *Appreciations of Japanese Culture* (Tokyo: Kodansha, 1981), 231.

18. Brinker, *Die zen-buddhistische Bildnismalerei,* 175.

19. Ibid., 79.

20. Seckel, *Jenseits des Bildes,* 62.

21. Ibid., 36.

Index

About the Authors

Heinrich Dumoulin holds a Ph.D. from the Gregorian University, Rome; a D. Litt. from the University of Tokyo; and an honorary Doctorate in Theology from the University of Wurzburg. A resident of Tokyo since 1935, he was Professor of Philosophy and History of Religions at Sophia University in Tokyo from 1941 to 1976. His writings include *Kamo Mabuchi: Ein Beitrag zur japanischen Reliogions- und Geistesgeschichte* (Tokyo, 1943); *The Development of Chinese Zen After the Sixth Patriarch* (New York, 1953); *A History of Zen Buddhism* (New York, 1963); *Östliche Meditation und christliche Mystik* (Freiburg, 1966); editor, *Buddhism in the Modern World* (New York, 1976); *Christianity Meets Buddhism* (La Salle, Illinois, 1974); *Zen Enlightenment* (Tokyo, 1979); *Zen Buddhism: A History,* 2 volumes (New York: Macmillan, 1988, 1990); *Zen Buddhism in the 20th Century* (New York, 1992), and many works in the Japanese language.

Joseph S. O'Leary, an Irish theologian, lectures in the Department of English Literature, Sophia University. He is the author of *Questioning Back: The Overcoming of Metaphysics in Christian Tradition* (New York: Harper & Row) and *Le Christianisme, les Religions et la vérité* (Paris: Editions du Cerf, 1994).

The "weathermark" identifies this book as a production of Weatherhill, Inc., publishers of fine books on Asia and the Pacific. Editorial supervision: Jeffrey Hunter. Production supervision: Bill Rose. Typography, book design and page composition: G & H Soho, Inc., Hoboken, New Jersey. Printing and Binding: Arcata Graphics, Fairfield, Pennsylvania. The typeface used is Fairfield, with Medici Script and Tiepolo for display.